Game Design Snacks

Game Design Snacks

Easily Digestible Game Design Wisdom

JOSÉ P. ZAGAL

CARNEGIE MELLON UNIVERSITY: ETC PRESS: STUDENT
PITTSBURGH, PA

Contents

Introduction   xi
What is this book about and how was it written?
José P. Zagal

Learning and Guiding

Tutorials Should Explain the Many Ways Mechanics Can Be Used   3
McKenna Caldwell

Showing Players an Enemy's Intent Can Encourage Tactical   5
Understanding
Kendal Kotter

Animation "Tells" Can Help Teach Players How To Play   7
McKenna Caldwell

Rewarding Highly Specific Uses of Moves Trains Players to Teach   9
Themselves Strategy
Benjamin Barker

Change and Consequences

Permanently Changing a Character's Appearance is Memorable   13
for Players
Lee Neuschwander

Players Feel Empowered when Actions in One Playthrough Affect   15
the Next
Benjamin Barker

Allow Characters to Grow (Narratively and Mechanically) from   17
Game to Game
Lee Neuschwander

AI that Reacts Credibly is Better than Super Smart AI   19
McKenna Caldwell

Failure

What Happens When you Die in a Game Influences What Players   23
do Next
Jacob Grahmann

Use Death Recaps to Teach Your Players How to Improve   25
Kendal Kotter

Perceptions of a Threat Work Better than the Threat in Creating   27
an Intense Experience
Jacob Grahmann

Foster Skilled Play by Encouraging Failure   29
Kendal Kotter

Movement and Navigation

Moving Between a Game's Areas Should Always be Memorable   33
Trevor Scott Richard

Guiding Players Indirectly is Better than Telling them Where to   35
Go
McKenna Caldwell

Use Shortcuts as Checkpoints to Give Players a Sense of   37
Discovery with Each Death
Benjamin Barker

Give Players a Traveling Companion to Help Introduce them to   39
Your Open World
McKenna Caldwell

Movement Mechanics Can Reinforce a Game's Core Experience   41
Trevor Scott Richard

Playstyles

Allowing Players to Switch Classes Encourages Exploration of   45
Game Mechanics
Jacob Grahmann

Including More Upgrade Options than Opportunities Leads to   47
More Replayability and Experimentation
Benjamin Barker

Collectibles can be Used to Encourage Diverse Playstyles   49
Trevor Scott Richard

Give Players a Toolbox and They'll Solve Puzzles of their Own   51
Devising
Jacob Grahmann

Unique and Challenging Achievements can Provide Players with   53
Motivation to Re-Visit Old Content
Lee Neuschwander

Let Your Players Customize Their Own Risk/Reward Ratios   55
Kendal Kotter

Variety in Gameplay

Randomized Character Names and Traits Can Lead to More   59
Engaging Experiences
Lee Neuschwander

Careful Repetition of Challenges Allows for Novel but Familiar   61
Player Experiences
Trevor Scott Richard

Repairable Weapon Degradation Encourages Weapon Use and   63
Reduces Hoarding
Lee Neuschwander

How to Do Drastic Gameplay Changes the Right Way   65
Kendal Kotter

Non-Violent Ways of Resolving Conflicts Makes Games More Interesting for Players   67
Jacob Grahmann

Being Overpowered Can Help Players Better Understand a Game   69
Kendal Kotter

User Interface and Visual Information

The User Interface Can Help the Player Share in their Character's Experience   73
Lee Neuschwander

Diegetic UI Helps the Player Care More About the Gameworld and its Characters   75
Benjamin Barker

Camera Perspectives Show/Obscure Info that Allow for Different Gameplay Challenges   77
Trevor Scott Richard

Fog of War Can Add to the Immersive Experience of a Game   79
Jacob Grahmann

Drawing Attention to Important Information in Multiple Ways Helps Players Understand Faster   81
McKenna Caldwell

Multi-Purpose Design

It is Often Better to Use One Button for Many Things   85
Trevor Scott Richard

Quick Time Events can be used to Build Tension and/or Empower Players   87
Jacob Grahmann

In-Game Collectables Should Have Purpose and Build Upon the Game   89
McKenna Caldwell

Reward Systems that Unite Gameplay and Story Support   91
Immersive Feedback Loops
Trevor Scott Richard

Playing with Others

Letting your Players be Nice to Each Other can Reduce Toxicity   95
Kendal Kotter
For Collaboration, Don't Let Players Talk to Each Other   97
Lee Neuschwander
Player Preferences Go Beyond Content and Gameplay   99
Jacob Grahmann
Change Player Movement Speed to Encourage Collaboration   101
José P. Zagal

Skilled Play

Hit Priority in Combat Systems Encourages Deeper and   105
Competitive Play
Jacob Grahmann
Use Skill Trees to Enrich Your Players' Skills   107
Kendal Kotter
Randomized Gun Spray Patterns Help Level the Playing Field for   109
Players
Benjamin Barker
Layer your Design to Achieve Both a Low Skill Floor and a High   111
Skill Ceiling
Kendal Kotter
Let Experienced Players Turn Off Breadcrumbs   113
Lee Neuschwander

Index of Games   115
About the Authors   121
About the ETC Press   123

Introduction

What is this book about and how was it written?

JOSÉ P. ZAGAL

They say that good design is invisible.

You don't notice when things are done "right", only when they are slightly off. One way to help us become more aware (and appreciative) of when things are done right in game design is to talk about them. To share them with others. This book is that sharing. We want to share with others small, easily digestible snippets of game design wisdom as seen in many of the commercially released video games we've played.

We call these nuggets of wisdom game design snacks.

The idea of a game design snack is inspired by Ernest Adams' "Bad Game Designer, No Twinkie!" columns. In these columns he described what he felt were egregious errors in game design. This book is similar, with each snack described in a few paragraphs and also supported by examples and (sometimes) illustrated with screenshots. Snacks are short and that's on purpose. They're supposed to be things to munch on, rather than a full-blown meal that will take time to fully digest.

As with many other things, the origin of this book has a story.

While the concept of a game design snack was inspired by Ernest Adams, it first saw life as a homework assignment.

I taught my first university-level game design course in the spring of 2000. Since then, I've had the opportunity to work with numerous students – all of them incredibly passionate and interested in games. Each student has a wealth of knowledge and experience with games that is different and unique from everyone else's. Maybe they had a game console that no one else liked, or they're fans of games in a certain genre. Despite this treasure trove of experiential knowledge, students don't always know how to articulate that knowledge such that it can be shared and made known more widely.

As an academic and researcher, I've been studying how to better help students use their experience with games so they can learn to talk and think about games as designers, rather than fans or gamers (see my book *Ludoliteracy*, also with ETC Press).

So, I've been asking students to write their own game design snacks as homework assignments for a few years now and this book represents a body of work that a handful of former students were excited about and wanted to refine. Many of the snacks in this book began as a homework assignment duly turned in for a grade. Starting in September of 2018, we looked at the snacks everyone had worked on, we picked the ones we felt were the most interesting and insightful, decided we needed to write up a few more, and got to work. We wrote. We iterated. We edited each other's work and we also talked about game design – a lot.

We hope you enjoy this book and the amazing games that are out there. More importantly, we would like to think that perhaps you might be inspired to write and share your own game design snacks.

LEARNING AND GUIDING

How do game designers help players better understand how to play their games?

Tutorials Should Explain the Many Ways Mechanics Can Be Used

MCKENNA CALDWELL

A game's tutorial should always strive to show players everything that a mechanic can do. This can encourage players to experiment with those mechanics in new and interesting ways. It can also help players remember what certain mechanics do and how they can apply them throughout the game.

In *Spider-Man*, the beginning tutorial is straightforward. It teaches the player basic mechanics for movement and combat in the game. Once learned, the game then introduces new ideas for using those same mechanics in different ways. A player needs to use the dodge mechanic to avoid being damaged by enemies, but if they dodge close to a wall, they will both avoid damage and bounce off the wall into the enemy: a dodge attack combo. The game has short messages that pop up on-screen to inform players that they can experiment. One tutorial teaches the player that they can shoot webs from Spider-man's web slingers to temporarily disable enemies. Then, when players use this mechanic, they can discover that when shooting the web at an enemy close to a wall, the enemy will become stuck to it and taken out of combat.

Great mechanics can be used in multiple ways and allow players to experiment. But they have to also be paired with tutorials that explain their multiple uses, and the scenarios where they could be handy. Many of the *Legend of Zelda* (LoZ) games have a hookshot: a tool that can be used to pull Link toward marked areas. Players can also learn that the hookshot can be used as a weapon. It kills some weak enemies instantly, and then pulls others toward Link, so that they are in range of the player's sword. The *LoZ* games encourage players to look around and try things to solve puzzles. They also use the hookshot's targeting to alert players to the fact that it can be used as both a weapon and a tool.

Games should strive to make tutorials fun and exciting, and designers should encourage players to experiment with the mechanics they are given in creative ways. But designers need to encourage experimentation and provide players with examples of the different ways a game's mechanics can be used.

Original snack idea by Josh Marchand.

Showing Players an Enemy's Intent Can Encourage Tactical Understanding

KENDAL KOTTER

Broadly speaking, designers should ensure that players understand what an enemy can do (or intends to do). At the very least, players should know the general range of actions that the enemy is capable of. But what happens if a player knows exactly what the enemy will do next? Initially, this might seem cheap and non-fun. Doesn't informing your player of what the enemy is about to do take all the suspense and skill out of the game? However, when used appropriately, knowing an enemy's intent actually makes the player's decisions and consequent actions more interesting – and can encourage players to understand the tactical nuances of a game's systems.

For example, *Into the Breach* is a turn-based strategy game that is based on the player knowing the enemies' exact moves. In other words, the player always knows exactly what the enemies will do in their next turn, from direction of attack, to how much damage, and so on. *Into the Breach* is an intentionally difficult game. It would likely be unbeatable for many players if this combat information were not given to the player. Also, since there will be no surprises (enemies will do exactly as communicated), failure in the game is squarely on the shoulders of the player. In a way, success in *Into the Breach* is akin to solving a puzzle – but here, the solution to the puzzle involves exploring the tactical possibilities of the game's system. For example, while I might not be able to avoid an enemy's attack, I might be able to push them into a location which renders the attack harmless. Or, I might even be able to push an enemy such that its impending attack harms another enemy. Exploring possible options to get out of a situation in which you have perfect information is a way to develop an understanding of a game's systems and how they interrelate.

Possible enemy actions are shown by the highlighted red squares (Into the Breach)

While *Into the Breach* was designed entirely around the idea of providing complete information to the player, this idea can also be applied in games in which an enemy's intent is obfuscated to increase tension and uncertainty. Most strategy and tactical games include a tutorial section – this can be an ideal context in which to show the player what enemies will do, to encourage them to find tactically-sound solutions. Gradually this information can be obfuscated, but by this time players will have developed the skills and understanding necessary to make informed decisions based on the enemies they see on the battlefield, and their knowledge of how they usually behave. The key takeaway is that it is important to help the player learn about the enemies, what they can do, and how they behave. Giving players explicit information about this is one way to do it. This can help players create their own mental models and understanding of the enemies in a game, as well as support them in making more informed – and yes, more strategic and skillful – decisions.

Original snack idea by Hunter Moffat.

Animation "Tells" Can Help Teach Players How To Play

MCKENNA CALDWELL

Animations in games can be used to give players information. The grass might be moving slightly to tell a player that the environment is windy. Or an enemy winding back its striking arm warns the player of an impending attack. The latter is an animation "tell" that informs the player of what an enemy is about to do so that the player can respond accordingly. Almost every game uses these tells and players rely on them to be successful.

Animation tells are crucial to playing any *Dark Souls* game. Without them, players wouldn't make it very far. All of the enemies in a *Dark Souls* game hit hard, and players must be quick to react in order to survive. When enemies attack, they have specific animations for those attacks. Sometimes fast or slow, animations will warn the player what kind of attack is coming, allowing them to react in the best way to avoid taking a hit. Learning and memorizing an enemy's tells is extremely important, especially when fighting powerful bosses. Counter attacks, for example, must be timed perfectly. However, they must be performed usually at the peak of an attack animation. When successful they can give a player a significant boost to the damage they inflict. Players have to carefully learn the attack animations of each enemy to know exactly where that window is, and it can sometimes mean the difference between life and death.

The Legend of Zelda Twilight Princess' (LoZ:TW) bosses all have specific tells to help the player know how to defeat them. The final boss of the game, Ganondorf, has multiple stages. The first, Ganon's Puppet Zelda, pits Link against a possessed Zelda who floats through the air wielding a sword. At certain moments, she will raise her sword towards the ceiling; an animation that tells the player what she will do next. If her sword begins to form a glowing yellow ball, this warns the player to be ready to strike back. If timed correctly, the player can wait for her to launch the glowing ball towards Link, then swing out with their own sword to "bat" the ball back towards her. The ball must be hit back and forth until eventually she will miss, resulting in her being damaged. If her sword rises but nothing forms, this warns players to dodge out of the way, as a damaging triforce will appear on the ground.

Ganon's Puppet Zelda raises her sword towards the ceiling and conjures a glowing orb thus warning the player of an impending attack (LoZ:TW)

Animation tells can help designers create organic player skill growth, helping them learn how to play the game, and play it well. Designers should strive to make creative and informative animations, using what is already present in the game, to help players be successful.

Original snack idea by Noah Harren.

Rewarding Highly Specific Uses of Moves Trains Players to Teach Themselves Strategy

BENJAMIN BARKER

How can you help players bridge the daunting skill gap that often separates casual players from those at a professional level? Designers will often include extensive tutorials to teach players high-level strategy. But these tutorials are not always effective because they are often text heavy or require repeated executions of the same button input to indicate that the player has "learned". To be fair, successfully teaching advanced strategies and techniques is challenging. However, this is where rewarding specific execution comes into play.

Imagine a move or ability that is simple to execute, but in certain (specific) circumstances, the player is rewarded with an extra effect (e.g. extra damage, restored resources, etc.). Thanks to the reward, the player is encouraged to understand the circumstances in which the reward happened, and they can thus begin to teach themselves the best uses for that move. When a game draws attention to high-level uses of a move, rather than communicating them directly, the player becomes empowered to figure things out by themselves and to search for further nuances.

Soulcalibur 6 does this with its "Lethal Hit" system. Each character has roughly ten basic moves which, when executed in specific circumstances, take on bonus effects such as dealing extra damage. One example of this is the character, Talim. She has a move called Isa Hampas in which she performs a short hop before slashing the enemy with her elbow blades. If this is done right after an enemy uses a low attack, she will jump over the enemy's low attack and the following slash will do extra damage. This teaches Talim players to look for enemy low attacks (to hop over and do extra damage) and also teaches players facing Talim to be cautious when performing low attacks against her (you are more vulnerable). *Soulcalibur 6*'s system has an additional layer of nuance – it also teaches players to look for moves with odd animations, such as Talim's little hop, which keys them into thinking that those moves may have uses or benefits that can be discovered or developed as advanced techniques.

Implementing a system such as this can be a great way to make the player feel like they are figuring out something clever, while also encouraging higher level strategies without risking one of the many problems that come with poorly designed tutorials such as walls of text, or the necessity of understanding every in-game system. Likewise, such an implementation can add longevity to the game, making each moment an opportunity for players to learn to utilize their moves' special uses, or to look for situations in which they can shine.

CHANGE AND CONSEQUENCES

How can players can become more invested in a game's world?

Permanently Changing a Character's Appearance is Memorable for Players

LEE NEUSCHWANDER

Allowing players to irreversibly change the appearance of their character in a game can be a powerful tool for its narrative impact, and it can greatly increase player enjoyability. The core idea is that providing opportunities in which a character's appearance irrevocably changes due to in-game events or player choices makes those events and choices much more memorable. Take getting a scar in real life (usually not the result of a choice); whatever it is that caused that scar can stay with you far more vividly than it would if no scar was left. The same can be said for a moment like that during a video game.

One such example occurs in *Bioshock Infinite*. There is a scene in the game where, while waiting for a bank teller to get back, you have the option to either take your hand off the counter or to leave it there. If you leave it there the bank teller comes back and pins your hand to the counter with a knife, and you have to go through the rest of the game with a bandage on your hand. If you were to make this exact choice in the game without it possibly permanently scarring the main character, the choice wouldn't be as memorable. As designed in the game, however, that moment can partially define your experience playing the game. It strengthens the sense of ownership towards the game's character and fosters a connection to the story. *Heavy Rain* is another game that does this well. In this game there is a dramatic moment in which the player must choose which fingers the protagonist should cut off. The protagonist is informed by the game's antagonist that he needs to show proof of his commitment to saving his kidnapped son by cutting off a finger in front of a camera that has been set up. Again, this moment is emotionally intense, and memorable, and, due to its irreversibility, the player must live with and bear witness to their decision for the duration of the game.

However, this isn't the only way that this design can be utilized. Game designers also often have the character change as a sign that the character is now at a different stage in their development. By having the character change in appearance, you are giving a visual indicator to the player of what they had to go through leading up to and after the change occurred. The change then acts as a visible memory for the player and greatly increases the level of impact that the moment had in the experience of playing the game. The important thing to note here is that the change must be permanent if it is to have the desired impact. If the player can simply change into something else or remove the mark at their leisure, it invalidates the imprinting effect upon the player; i.e. if you got a cool jacket for a big choice you made, the memory will only last until you get another jacket. However, if you end up taking away the player's arm that will create a much stronger memory.

Players Feel Empowered when Actions in One Playthrough Affect the Next

BENJAMIN BARKER

In most games the character's actions (usually chosen by the player) affect the gameworld, and these changes stop when the game is finished. Some developers have employed systems that allow actions in one playthrough to have visible effects on the next. This should not to be confused with "new game plus", which is a game mode that is unlocked when you first finish a game and allows players to play again with the characters, items and experience earned from their first playthrough. Allowing follow-up playthroughs of a game to be shaped by actions during a previous playthrough can affect the player's level of immersion, as it requires the game to communicate with the player that it knows it is a game. However, this is an extremely effective way of delivering an empowering experience for players. With this, the game transcends its traditional limits by recognizing that the player exists outside of the character. For developers searching to truly immerse their players, the idea of the "power fantasy" is a common and reliable design pillar that is realized here with players having power and agency beyond a single playthrough of a game.

There are few examples of this type of game design, but those that exist frequently find cult status among fans due to their dramatic changes to expected gameplay loops. *Doki Doki Literature Club* is one such example. On the first playthrough, players reach a point in which one of the main characters dies. The game then presents a "game over" message and the player is returned to the title screen. However, when players play the game a second time, they will notice that the dead character is absent from all in-game art (e.g. where normally they appeared on the title screen). When players proceed into their second playthrough, every line of dialogue the deceased character had the first time around is replaced with an unsettling string of glitch text. The game also has an interesting mechanic that allows players to access, alter and delete, its character files. If players choose to do so, the game will respond on subsequent launches with messages and events that make it clear that the game is aware of the player's actions. Here, players realize that their actions have effects that are more significant and powerful than what they expected, resulting in an experience of empowerment.

Designing subsequent playthroughs to be affected by the first can be a daunting task. For developers with limited resources, another way of achieving a similar effect is to let the player think that their actions are affecting later plays, when they actually aren't. A game that employs this strategy is *The Stanley Parable*. During each play of the game, certain objects (chairs, boxes, etc.) are randomized in their location and orientation. Since the game is about player choice and the strange effects this has on the world, players often ascribe meaning to these random events and convince themselves that they are responsible for the lights being out in the office or for stray paint lines on the floors and walls.

Designing a gameplay experience to reflect a player's choices from previous playthroughs is an extremely powerful tool. It should be noted that these changes are only noticeable on replays of the game, so the initial playthrough ought to require an investment of a short period of time in order to get to that payoff in the first place. Both *Doki Doki Literature Club* and *The Stanley Parable* can be finished in short sessions: a few hours and minutes respectively. This not only prevents the player from feeling daunted, but it also lightens the workload immensely, compared to single playthrough 60+ hour games.

Original snack idea by Yuqi Shi.

Allow Characters to Grow (Narratively and Mechanically) from Game to Game

LEE NEUSCHWANDER

Across the game industry, stand-alone titles are becoming less frequent. If any modicum of success is seen from an individual title, a sequel – and often, a series – is born. Common elements from the first game are often carried through to the next: important characters, narrative plot lines, game mechanics, and more. This carry-through of game content across a series grants developers a chance to evolve these characters, plotlines and mechanics. In turn, this evolution brings opportunities to increase player immersion, strengthen ludonarrative harmony through intertwined narrative and mechanic progression, and maintain and strengthen player buy-in. All of this is perhaps most effective when applied to playable characters due to their direct connection to the player.

Portraying playable characters as evolving figures across a series is a tricky act to balance. If done right, players will be more likely to feel invested in the game's characters, and feel a part of the game itself. If done poorly, players will feel disconnected or uninvolved in the game. Players might even feel betrayed if the character changes in ways perceived as too extreme or contrary to the original character.

One way for having characters evolve is to show character progression and development over each individual game through narrative and game mechanic changes. Ideally, the player is involved in the character progression (directly or indirectly). It's important to note that this character progression can't simply be a result of graphic or hardware improvement: purely aesthetic changes are easy, but true narrative and mechanic progression is immensely more satisfying.

Across the three main games of *The Witcher* series, Geralt (the playable character) grows from a young, emotionless man to a grizzled, unsure-of-himself aged man. This is reflected in his look (he physically ages and becomes more scarred), his narrative/dialogue (he slowly becomes much more introspective and questioning about his place in the world), and the gameplay mechanics (as he opens up emotionally across the series, more dialogue options with more narrative weight are available to the player). This example of character progression is well done because it takes place gradually over the course of a series, involves the player in narrative choices that signify the character's growth and changes, and enhances these narrative changes through a variety of gameplay changes.

The 2013 version of *Tomb Raider* is another example of this type of character growth. Over the course of *Tomb Raider*, *Rise of the Tomb Raider*, and *Shadow of the Tomb Raider*, Lara Croft grows from an inexperienced explorer to a rough, grizzled adventurer that knows her way around a gun. Her looks change, her in-game abilities become more complex and advanced as her character does (evolving mechanics tied to character progression), and her narrative options reflect her transition from timid and afraid to more decisive and action-forward options. The character progression is successful not because of any one of these factors, but because of all of them.

As a player character grows over the course of a series, players can connect more strongly with that character, and thus connect more strongly with the series as a whole. This not only benefits the series by creating more devoted fans, it also allows for more impactful narrative experiences. By allowing players to feel as if they're having significant influence on the game itself (the act of them playing is evolving the character, thus inserting themselves into the narrative, in a sense), developers can orchestrate situations where the game's narrative can have greater impact on the players themselves.

AI that Reacts Credibly is Better than Super Smart AI

MCKENNA CALDWELL

Designing intelligent AI can be tricky. Players like to be challenged by enemies that aren't just bullet fodder or pose no real threat. However, players can feel cheated when AI is too smart and seems to play the game better than they can. AI seems to be best when it is somewhere in the middle. Not stupid, but not truly intelligent either. What becomes important then is making the player believe that the AI is intelligent by having it react in ways that are credible but that can be anticipated by the player. This makes players feel like they outsmarted the game, when in reality, it was all a part of the design.

In combat situations, the AI in *The Last of Us* reacts to what the player is doing and adjusts accordingly. If a player decides not to stay in cover and moves right into the fray brandishing their gun, the AI enemies will back off, often running away or shooting from cover themselves. If a player stays in cover and tries to slowly pick off the enemy, the AI will occasionally try to flank the player or move forward when the player has to reload. The AI doesn't immediately take the smartest route. Rather, it waits for the player to show their hand, and then takes a route that, to the player, is seen as "smart". This makes the AI feel real to the player. In this way, AI can present real challenges if a player doesn't take in a situation correctly, leaving them open. In many ways, it's tricking the player into feeling they have outwitted a truly worthy foe.

In *Alien: Isolation*, the xenomorph is the main enemy. Abandoned on a ship, players find themselves checking every corner for the giant alien. Instead of following a set invisible path in every level or stage of the ship, the alien responds to sound and sight. This sense-based AI will search areas where it hears noises or catches glimpses of the player. This makes the alien seem unpredictable, and gives the player the sense that it can come out at any moment. As in *The Last of Us*, this AI only reacts to what the player does, rather than being truly autonomous. If a player makes a loud sound or doesn't get into cover fast enough, the alien will follow them or even look right into the locker they hid inside. It increases the immersion of the game, making every situation feel frightfully unsafe. Furthermore, the xenomorph "learns" from past player behavior – so, it learns from what the player does most often and reacts accordingly. Players have to be aware of everything they do, and try to gauge what the alien might hear or see. This can also make players feel like they have control over situations, and give them opportunities to outsmart the alien AI.

Players can hide from the alien but must stay quiet to avoid being found (Alien: Isolation)

AI that seem intelligent can also make a game feel more immersive and intense. When characters and enemies seem like they have human-like reactions and decision making, the world can feel more real. This can push players to think harder and encourage them to be more creative and think situations through, which can lead to more rewarding victories. But the best kind of smart AI is one that will only be as good as the player, pushing them, but not destroying them.

FAILURE

How do game designers help players benefit from their own failures?

What Happens When you Die in a Game Influences What Players do Next

JACOB GRAHMANN

Dying in a game is usually a sign of failure. Something went wrong, don't worry, try again. However, it's not that simple. Consider permadeath, one of the players' worst enemies – or is it? In video games, permanent death is a game mechanic, wherein a player must restart a game, losing all progress made when their character dies or is eliminated. Losing all progress is a high price to pay, especially in a game that may last tens of hours. What value is there to adding permadeath to a game you may ask?

Well, it forces the players to think critically about their decisions before they act. By adding permadeath to a game, designers create an experience that favors strategy instead of reckless action. As a tool, it encourages players to weigh their decisions carefully before they act. After all, the cost of failure can be high in terms of time and effort invested.

However, when implemented poorly it can spoil a game. In games where players are expected to spend tens of hours developing and progressing their characters, permadeath can quickly lead to player frustration, especially if the death occurred due to circumstances outside of the player's control. For example, an unlucky die roll that the player cannot prepare for, or mitigate. As a mechanic, permadeath highlights the consequences of a player's decisions – and as such, when it occurs, it should ideally be due to mistakes made by the player.

Games in the *Dark Souls* series find an interesting middle ground between the severity of permadeath and player failure of little consequence. In *Dark Souls* games, *Souls* are the main currency. They are used to level up and buy items, and are essential to making progress in the game. When the player's character dies, they drop all of the souls they have collected. When the player's character respawns, they have one chance to return to where they died to retrieve the *Souls*. Players get one shot at avoiding the consequences of failure. It is an interesting balance in which players must carefully consider their actions and must develop their skills to avoid prior mistakes. It also gives players a strong and clear motivation to continue playing: recover what you earned before it is gone forever! Losing all the *Souls* might have been too frustrating for players, and simply respawning without any loss would have discouraged the kind of careful and cautious player experience the designers desired.

So, what happens when you die in a game can really influence what the player does next. Will they be motivated to try again or will they give up in frustration? Death mechanics are a key component of a game's design and can affect player experience to the same degree that movement and interaction do. This is why so much attention should be given to creating a death system that is tailored specifically for your game. By having a carefully designed death system that complements and supports a game's other mechanics, designers are able to encourage players to grow or achieve their desired gameplay experience.

Use Death Recaps to Teach Your Players How to Improve

KENDAL KOTTER

Death recaps are becoming an increasingly important feature in modern games. In general, death recaps are activated immediately after a player has died in a game, and show the players a replay of how they died and what precisely caused their death. Some games' death recaps communicate more detailed data to the players, such as damage numbers and percentage breakdowns. Although featured most prominently in first-person shooter games such as *Overwatch* and *PlayerUnknown's Battlegrounds* (PUBG), death recaps also have a place and purpose in more single-player centric titles.

A death recap is often thought of as nothing more than a time filler used to occupy the attention of the player while they wait to respawn or restart a level. However, when used appropriately and communicated to the player clearly, death recaps can allow players to learn in ways they otherwise might not. In first-person shooter games such as *Overwatch*, death recaps allow players to see the game from a perspective they otherwise would not be able to. By seeing their character's death through the eyes of the enemy, players can learn such things as proper positioning, map awareness, creative mechanic usages, effective teamwork plays, and more. In a single-player environment, such as *Super Meat Boy*, death recap allows players to see exactly where they went wrong in the level. *Super Meat Boy* shows players how they have died every single time and then leaves the dead bodies of prior attempts within the level permanently, thereby allowing players to see exactly where they failed in the past and (hopefully) avoid failing there in the future. By providing players with information about the mistakes they made, they're able to learn and grow from those mistakes instead of simply repeating them.

Allowing the player to re-witness their death is not necessarily enough to support learning. The information given in death recaps needs to be appropriate and trimmed down to the essentials. Death recaps are designed to be short, informing the player of what caused their death and then quickly getting them back into the game. If the wrong information is conveyed during this time, or if too much information is given to the player too quickly, death recaps can easily become a hindrance or a nuisance instead of a guide to the players. Consider what information is essential for your particular game and genre, and then find out how you can get that information across in the most concise, but effective way possible. As with all things game development, playtesting your death recap system will be imperative.

Death recaps have primarily been designed and used in FPS games. However, the benefits of death recaps aren't genre specific and, as in the case of *Super Meat Boy*, can significantly improve the game as a whole.

Perceptions of a Threat Work Better than the Threat in Creating an Intense Experience

JACOB GRAHMANN

You are walking through a dark hallway and hear noise behind you. Panic sets in, and you turn around to find nothing there. Games in the horror genre often use the element of a constant threat to give players the feeling of being on edge, even when their character is not in danger. Many horror games create this atmosphere through the use of enemies that are unable to be removed during gameplay. When in-game enemies cannot be defeated by the players, players will tend to seek to avoid the threats to the best of their abilities. Knowing this, developers can use this information against the player by using noises or visuals during low-energy portions of the game to create tension and evoke emotion – the player thinks there is danger, but there often isn't. By implementing these tactics developers can cause the game to evoke powerful emotions within the player, such as fear, dread, loneliness, anxiety and doubt. These powerful emotions, combined with a constant threat, is what makes these types of horror games effective at keeping players afraid.

A game that implements this well is *SCP – Containment Breach*. The game revolves around an organization which perform tests on monsters (called SCPs) to determine what they do. They also use convicted criminals on death row, and you play as one of them. The game uses the monster's abilities, paired with the characters unfortunate circumstances, to evoke powerful emotions of fear within the player. In the game, some SCP's appear as regular objects that, when approached, cause a terrible death. The uncertainty about what is safe in the environment causes players to feel nervous and on edge when interacting with objects and items in the environment. The game also allows some SPC's to move between rooms randomly. The uncertainty in what the player will encounter in the next room, or the room prior, adds to the intensity of the emotions felt by the player.

Silent Hill 2 is another example. Here, the player must search a town for clues to return home. The game features an aggressive non-player entity named Pyramid Head that relentlessly pursues the player around the map as they progress through the game. The developers use the noise of Pyramid Head's knife dragging across the ground, along with the sounds of him choking, to create a sense of urgency and fear, even if Pyramid Head hasn't caught up to the player. Pyramid Head is used to encourage the player to move through the game without spending too much time in one area, thus adding a sense of urgency to the fear the player already feels.

When implementing perceptions of threats, it is important to balance the amount of time the player encounters the actual threat. If the threat is never encountered – then the perceptions turn into false alarms that won't be effective. If a player encounters the threat too often, it can quickly lose its novelty making the game unsurprising, thus minimizing the emotional effect on the player. By using noises or visuals to cause the player's imagination to work against them, many powerful emotions can be generated in players, with little work. As the saying goes, sometimes less is more.

Original snack idea by Robert Park

Foster Skilled Play by Encouraging Failure

KENDAL KOTTER

Failure in video games is an essential concept: you can't win a game if you can't also lose that same game. From a cursory glance, that failure has a negative connotation. If the player's goal is to win the game, then doesn't anything that impedes that goal also restrict the player's agency and enjoyment of the game? Obviously that answer is no, but here is one reason why.

Failure provides a contrast to success. Players are able to have a more enjoyable experience completing a level after having failed that level, precisely because that contrast increases the value of their success. But failure is more than just a method of contrasting success; it's also a signifier of growth. Once a player fails, it allows them to see the game in a new light. It forces them to reconsider how they were playing, as well as analyze their play to discover what they need to change. When failure is implemented fairly and correctly into a game, players will enjoy failing to a certain extent, precisely because it allows them to grow and overcome their mistakes. Passing a point where a player once failed shows the player that they've learned from their mistakes.

The challenging part is implementing moments of failure that feel fair to your player, and help them to become more skilled at the game itself. To achieve this, be certain that your failure states are clearly communicated to your player. Players will quickly become frustrated when they encounter failure states, and are unaware of the preceding events, or failure states that feel random or arbitrary. Also, be certain to appropriately balance the punishment for the failure state. Generally, difficult gameplay is compensated with lighter fail states (i.e. checkpoints placed right after difficult sections, so that players don't have to repeat their previous accomplishments). Although this rule can be broken under some circumstances, be careful: if a player feels that their failure is too punitive, it can quickly destroy that player's motivation to play the game.

For a series that utilizes failure appropriately while still being challenging, study *Dark Souls* and its sequels. The gameplay in *Dark Souls* is incredibly difficult for a purpose. It teaches players how to play the game at a higher level, thus allowing them to progress. Because players repeat sections of the game so frequently due to death, players learn to master each section. Players also gain an increased awareness of their surroundings in-game, learn how to better maximize their combos and fight patterns, and learn how to anticipate enemy actions. Each of these elements is then utilized throughout the rest of the game so players don't feel like their time and effort was wasted. The difficulty of *Dark Souls* works because players understand what led to their failures, they understand what they need to improve to reduce their failures, and they feel appropriately rewarded for overcoming their failures.

Let players fail in your game. Depending on the difficulty level of your game, let them fail often. However, make sure that those failures have a purpose, and that that purpose is helping your player become better at playing the game. As always, playtesting your game will be essential here. Make sure that you playtest the game with your target audience.

MOVEMENT AND NAVIGATION

What do game designers do to make moving around game worlds more interesting?

Moving Between a Game's Areas Should Always be Memorable

TREVOR SCOTT RICHARD

As open-world designs that allow for non-linear exploration have become more popular, videogame players increasingly find themselves retreading familiar regions in their favorite games. Oftentimes, this means the price of large-scale and complex level design is increased navigational tedium: travelling around gets boring. Let's look at some of the ways game designers address this problem.

Some players complain that backtracking is a primary source of boredom in games that emphasize exploration. In an attempt to alleviate this problem, some designers do their best to eliminate the phenomenon. Common solutions include providing fast travel systems, or crafting clever shortcuts through the map, thereby allowing the player to move more quickly between areas. When done well, these efforts can result in a game with a world that feels more immediately engaging than it would otherwise. However, this isn't always the best approach. In many cases, systems that allow the player to avoid backtracking can actually make exploring a game's world less interesting. With environments as beautiful as those in titles like *Metroid* or *Dark Souls* – both series in which getting lost is central to the game experience – over-implementation of shortcuts and fast travel might allow players to, as *Civilization IV* designer Soren Johnson put it, "optimize the fun out of a game".

However, it is possible to remove tedium from exploration by making the backtracking itself more engaging. *Castlevania: Symphony of the Night* features a handful of fast travel points littered throughout its vast map – just enough to make backtracking manageable without eliminating the need to revisit old areas entirely. When players do backtrack, however, they will rarely be bored because they'll often be given the opportunity to explore previously inaccessible areas with newly acquired power-ups. Even when the player is totally lost and wandering aimlessly, *Symphony of the Night*'s basic movement and combat mechanics are compelling enough to keep them engaged. The best modern "Metroidvanias" apply these lessons so that traversing their worlds over and over again is actually interesting, rather than just tedious or confusing.

The next time you find yourself lost in a video-game, or spending a lot of time backtracking, think about what the designers have (or have not) done to make that experience engaging. If the game has an overly generous fast travel system, consider temporarily ignoring it as a sort of experiment. Does revisiting previously explored areas feel meaningful? Is simply getting from place to place a chore? These and other such questions will help you to consider how we navigate virtual spaces, and how designers can encourage players to do so in interesting and intentional ways.

Original snack idea by Jay Payne.

Guiding Players Indirectly is Better than Telling them Where to Go

MCKENNA CALDWELL

In the game, *Journey*, players have one goal: reach the mountain seen in the distance. The game doesn't use any dialogue or words to tell the player that is their goal. At the start of the game, players spawn in the middle of a sprawling desert. Once they climb the top of a sand dune, they can see a mountain in the distance, its peak split by a glowing light beam. It might be a little obvious, but players are then instantly aware that is where they need to go. It's almost always present, standing out and guiding players in the right direction.

The mountain in the distance in *Journey* is what is referred to as a "weenie". The term was used by Walt Disney, when he discovered that he could guide his dog to a certain part of his house by waving a hot dog. He then incorporated this idea into his theme park design, by using visually interesting tall structures to stimulate the curiosity of park-goers, and guide them towards different areas in the park. Weenies can be a variety of things in video games, basically anything that is a part of the environment that can be used as a guide for where to go and what to do. Lighting, objects and sounds can all be used as indirect guides through a game. They can be subtle or obvious, but when designed effectively, they can make a player feel smart by giving them the feeling they figured out something they weren't specifically told.

The mountain seen in the distance is almost always visible as a guide (Journey)

God of War uses many types of weenies, including tall mountains, creatures, sounds and lights to guide players through its world. The game uses light in clever ways that, while obvious when pointed out, feel natural to the player. In one area, the players are subtly guided towards an archway. A bright light, or "god ray", shines through and the archway is very slightly triangular with an intricately-carved arrowhead above it that fits in with the area's art style. The light is the most guiding weenie in this case, offsetting the dark interior of the room. It is both subtle and obvious, but using the environment as a guide in this way lessens the need for mission pointers and map markers.

Weenies don't always have to be tall objects. Designers can use context clues, made from different game elements, lighting, sound and environments, to lead players through their games in ways that feel natural. Doing this can increase a player's feeling of immersion because it makes them feel like they are their own guides. Players feel good about exploring and then realize that yes, they are indeed making progress and heading towards interesting places and things.

Original snack idea by Yuqi Shi.

Use Shortcuts as Checkpoints to Give Players a Sense of Discovery with Each Death

BENJAMIN BARKER

While they come in a large variety, checkpoints are generally described as locations where, once reached, the player character will respawn on subsequent deaths. They became a staple in games for good reason; giving the players a sense of progress is key to retaining their interest for a long or particularly difficult experience. They are a wonderful thing for linear games with a high skill requirement, but for games with other design pillars, traditional checkpoints aren't the most useful game asset.

One variation of checkpoints is to let shortcuts serve the same function. Rather than respawning at a checkpoint, the player must travel to the location of their death. However, this is faster than usual because they can use a shortcut that only became available when the player reached the far location. For example, there might be a locked door that can be used later once it has been unlocked from the other side. Using shortcuts in this way heightens the sense of exploration as it teaches players to become attentive to their environment. This is particularly effective in games that already emphasize exploration.

While shortcuts used in this manner are not literal checkpoints (the player does not spawn at the shortcut itself), this type of level design offers opportunities that a more traditional checkpoint system would not. When players die and respawn in their regular position or even at the start of the level, opening a shortcut not only rewards the player for their progress, but changes the level in a manner that can only be appreciated after a death (unlocking a shortcut won't matter if the character doesn't die to be sent back prior to the shortcut).

Shortcuts are used as checkpoints in *Dark Souls*, and is something that its many copycats don't often emulate. One example can be found in the area called "Undead Burg". Whenever players die here they are sent back to the bonfire (a literal checkpoint). This bonfire is directly in front of a highly dangerous bridge. Once players pass the bridge, they will enter a dark building, and then exit to find a series of twisting staircases, crossbow snipers, and undead zombies. However, once the player reaches the tower toward the end of the level (where the boss resides), they can unlock a door that will allow them to quickly skip from the bridge to the tower after failed encounters with the boss. This door opens from the dark building mentioned earlier.

This use of shortcuts not only rewards players for their progress, but makes their deaths an experience for discovery. The areas that the player skips via the shortcut then become mostly unvisited. Because of this, when players do make their way into these newly-optional areas, the once-mundane spaces become new again, thereby increasing the longevity of each level. This dynamic novelty to the levels teaches players that each area can be viewed in interesting ways, and pushes them to look for further hidden passageways and alternate routes, thereby heightening the sense of awe and discovery that the player experiences even within levels that might not have any shortcuts at all.

Original snack idea by Mario Gonzales.

Give Players a Traveling Companion to Help Introduce them to Your Open World

MCKENNA CALDWELL

Open world games can sometimes feel daunting to new players. Where should they go? Why should they want to go somewhere? Many games use non-diegetic techniques to help players. For example, an on-screen prompt that indicates a direction to head in, or a tutorial section that heavy-handedly orders the player around.

Another solution is to invite the player into the world in a way that can feel more natural and authentic: have an in-game character travel with the player's character. They can show the player around, point out interesting locations and provide narrative tidbits and possible goals for players to pursue; an early in-game character that can play the role of an unofficial tour guide, if you will.

Skyrim does this well. The world in *Skyrim* is vast, and once a player has access to the world map they can feel overwhelmed. To combat this, in an early scene in the game, the player chooses a non-player character as a companion. This character leads players to Riverwood, one of the game's first towns. While en route to Riverwood, the player can talk to their companion and learn more about the world and its major political players. The player's travelling partner (curiously) happens to have relatives in Riverwood who are hospitable, generous and helpful in suggesting the character's next destination: the city of Whiterun, a location that is centrally located in Skyrim, and an ideal location from which to then journey out into the world.

These early quests and the traveling companion are an excellent gentle introduction into the otherwise overwhelming size of Skyrim. By providing an early traveling companion, the player can learn about the story and themes of the game in a more natural way. These early quests introduce the player to the open and free nature of the game. The player learns that there is much they can explore and discover on their own, but subtly hint at how to best go about doing it (e.g. the city of Whiterun makes for an excellent area to travel out from and then return to regroup). This approach is also surprisingly not restrictive, as the vastness of the gameworld is not really blocked off from the player, it just seems impolite to abandon your companion.

Designing a game such that the introduction to the open world is guided by an in-game character companion allows games to have both story and world without feeling like sacrificing one or the other. And it can help early exploration feel natural to new players, while also making the "tutorial" moments of the game feel interesting and less like a tutorial.

Movement Mechanics Can Reinforce a Game's Core Experience

TREVOR SCOTT RICHARD

The way a game's basic movement mechanics feel is often the first and most important impression a player will get of the game. As our society's rapidly improving technology encourages consumers to increasingly expect intuitive and convenient means of interfacing with new products, many players carry similar expectations into their experiences with video-games. If a game initially appears to be unnecessarily difficult or otherwise unwieldy to control, some players won't even give it a second chance. However, while it is generally true that game designers should strive for controls that are easy to learn and immediately enjoyable, there are moments in which a less conventional approach yields more interesting results.

Perhaps no individual game designer is a better case study for intentionally unintuitive controls schemes than indie developer, Bennett Foddy, creator of *Getting Over It*. The game is about appreciating difficulty and frustration for their own sake. Accordingly, *Getting Over It* features a bare-bones movement system in which the player makes progress by tediously flicking their mouse around as their legless character tries to scale a mountain with nothing more than a sledgehammer. As the player bumbles toward their nigh-unreachable goal, they are accompanied by voice-over recordings of Foddy waxing philosophical about the nature of struggle and loss. If that isn't ludonarrative harmony, then I don't know what is.

It isn't just high-minded indie devs using unfriendly movement mechanics to reinforce a game's themes or setting; certain survival-horror games are classic examples of this technique. The original *Resident Evil* subverts player expectations with unforgivingly obtuse controls. The game limits mobility by making even the simple act of turning around difficult. Players must use the controller's shoulder buttons to rotate their character before moving forward or backward with the D-pad. This control scheme can be frustrating enough on its own, but it becomes downright panic-inducing when it's your only way to escape from an enemy that you don't have the health or ammo to face. Although this system might be understood merely as an artifact of the original PlayStation controller, which didn't have a joystick, we can also appreciate the way it contributes to the overall experience of *Resident Evil*. The game's unconventionally unintuitive controls allow its horrifying narrative to be reflected in its basic movement mechanics. This and other similarly surprising ideas are a big part of what makes classic survival horror so unique. Games like *Resident Evil* and *Silent Hill* don't just have scary stories; playing them is frightening in and of itself.

Of course, a game's movement mechanics don't have to be particularly difficult in order to be unique or contribute to the game's core experience. Consider the unusually floaty and imprecise platforming of *Little Big Planet*, which reinforces the game's lighthearted and handcrafted aesthetic; or think about how the differences in movement speed reflect the priorities of arena shooters like *Halo* or *Doom*, vs more "realistic" shooters inspired by games like *Call of Duty*. The general principle at work in all of these examples is that even something as fundamental as a game's basic movement systems presents an important opportunity to explore and reiterate a game's central ideas – whether those ideas are mechanically or narratively oriented. Just be sure not to overlook games that do this using uncommon or off-putting controls. Oftentimes, it's these unconventional cases which ultimately prove to be the most instructive and the most interesting.

PLAYSTYLES

What do game designers do to encourage players to play games in different ways?

Allowing Players to Switch Classes Encourages Exploration of Game Mechanics

JACOB GRAHMANN

Many MMORPGs today have fixed class systems where, at the beginning of the game, you decide the class of your character, which determines your skills and gear types for the rest of the game. The downside to these fixed class systems is that they limit player creativity. In order to experience another class the player must make a new character and start from scratch. This can be problematic for players already invested in the game, because they must now progress through the game again in order to be able to enjoy the second character as much as their first. This results in many players sticking to one character with one class, thus missing out on experiencing all of the game content. This can be resolved by implementing changeable builds.

A game with changeable builds (including items and skills) helps players to experience different kinds of gameplay without wasting time on leveling up. Games that implement changeable builds often allow player characters to equip any item in the game, the items determining the class and abilities your character has. Other games implement changeable builds by allowing the player to spend money or experience points to change classes. By implementing this mechanic, the game allows players to have more freedom and creativity when exploring the mechanics and tools given to them.

An example of this is seen in *Tom Clancy's The Division* where the player's class is determined from items held in the player's inventory, and which skills the player has equipped. This means the player can be any class they want, if they have the right items. So, a player wanting to serve as a medic in their team could equip the First Aid, Support Station, and Recovery Link skills to heal injured and downed comrades, and use an assault rifle that can inflict damage from a distance, while remaining close enough to use the support skills. A player wanting to emphasize damage, or draw enemy attention from teammates would equip different skills and weapons.

If you want players to explore all of the mechanics of your game, allowing a changeable build is important for encouraging your players to do so.

Original snack idea by Hao Qin.

Including More Upgrade Options than Opportunities Leads to More Replayability and Experimentation

BENJAMIN BARKER

Game designers regularly keep players actively engaged by letting them unlock character abilities gradually. A common loop is: player executes desired action, gains experience points, spends a bulk of experience to unlock a given ability, this ability allows them to more efficiently execute future desired actions. Many games will allow players to earn enough experience points (or whatever the unlock currency/method may be) to gain every possible upgrade. Developers do this to give players a sense of accomplishment, but often fail to realize that they are underselling both the game and player alike.

A tactic to aid replayability is to provide less of the given upgrade currency than players would need to unlock all their characters' abilities. This results in the players having to choose certain upgrade routes, varying them with each playthrough. The bigger the gap between player currency available and amount required to reach the maximum level, the higher the replay value, as it will take more plays to see all that the game has to offer.

A commonly overlooked upside of this design choice is that players, knowing a playthrough will only result in limited upgrade currency, will actually often try out greater and more varied skill loadouts with each play. This is because, with a lower number of experience points, the possibilities are easier for a player to calculate, thereby allowing them to more easily entertain the idea of varied paths. This careful consideration results in players ascribing a greater sense of value to each new skill. A common byproduct of designing in this manner is that skills will often have more power than their equivalent in a high-income game might have. Because the player is upgrading less often, the skills will have a higher power level to compensate.

While all of these effects are indeed generally positive, incorporating such a system can lead to a danger of which designers ought to be wary: with higher potency/more varied skills, yet limited income, first time players run the risk of upgrading to a new skill which they come to learn is not what they expected or is less useful than they anticipated. At its least intrusive, this is mildly frustrating to a player, and at its worst, this can be infuriating to the point that a player turns off the game and stops playing altogether. To avoid this, it is recommended that designers include clear descriptions of new skills' properties, and perhaps even a method that will allow players to re-spec (undo their skill choices, allowing them to choose differently) if they do not enjoy their chosen direction.

Dishonored has a system of unlockable and upgradable skills. These abilities tend to be stealth or damage based. This dual-minded approach encourages players to try each route. These skills are made available with the collection of runes. However, there are a limited number of runes throughout each level. This results in players tending to choose one of the broad playstyles over the other within a single setting. Because of this, players should play the game a second time in order to fully understand the available skills.

Original snack idea by McKenna Caldwell.

Collectibles can be Used to Encourage Diverse Playstyles

TREVOR SCOTT RICHARD

Calibrating a game's difficulty to appeal to players of all skill-levels is a real challenge; that exhilarating sense of flow players sometimes experience is only possible when a game is neither too easy nor too hard, and the position and size of this 'goldilocks zone' will vary wildly from person to person. Traditionally, designers have gotten around this variability in skill by allowing the player to select from various difficulty modes before beginning their game. While this solution has clear benefits, it also has significant drawbacks – chief among them is the fact that player skill comes in an innumerable assortment of flavors. A better way to address the problem of skill variability is to design games that offer a variety of collectibles, each with different playstyles and degrees of associated difficulty. This allows players to repeatedly and intuitively select their desired difficulty level over the full course of a playthrough, as they choose which collectibles to pursue and which to ignore. Of course, the success of this approach frequently depends on how well a game's designers have implemented its collectibles.

A game's main objectives are generally much easier to reach than its collectibles, as is the case with *Super Mario Odyssey*. The game offers 836 unique power moons for players to collect, but it only requires about a seventh of that amount in order to rescue Princess Peach. This means that younger or less obsessive players are able to beat the game with comparatively little trouble, while those looking for more are kept happy for dozens of hours collecting all the moons. It isn't the mere quantity of this game's collectibles that makes them so effective, though. Nintendo's secret sauce in their recipe for all-ages fun is their persistent ability to engage players with a variety of playstyles. Some of *Odyssey*'s power moons require a technically demanding series of jumps to reach, while others reward patient and thorough exploration. There are moons awarded for traversing an area quickly, and moons given out by NPCs who want Mario to help them find the right ingredients for their stew. The list goes on; no matter what it is about Mario's adventure with Cappy that you find most interesting or accessible, there's plenty for you to see and do. The 'goldilocks zone' of flow is a moveable feast in this wacky and wonderful game.

Super Mario Odyssey stands in stark contrast to more traditionally trendy open-world games overstuffed with a plethora of content just to justify the price tag. Content for content's sake doesn't guarantee an engaging experience; it is the quality and variety of a game's content that makes it worth playing for hundreds of hours, not its quantity.

Whenever a game includes lots of collectibles, the variability should come along with differences in terms of difficulty. Some should be easier to collect, and others harder. Also, they should challenge players' skills in different ways. Players of such games need not become overwhelmed by completionism or feel obligated to play on ultra-nightmare mode just to prove they can do it. It's always valuable to ask why the designers chose to include the content they did, and whether pursuing the game's various goals actually feels worthwhile. Critically evaluating the tasks that video-games ask us to perform will help players and designers alike to spend more energy on content that is truly engaging, and less on that which is merely plentiful.

Give Players a Toolbox and They'll Solve Puzzles of their Own Devising

JACOB GRAHMANN

Many games seek to have the player feel clever by solving a puzzle or executing a particular sequence of events. While these design choices have their merits, such methods can force the player to play in a manner they might not prefer. One way to have the player use their head without forcing them into unwanted methods of play is to provide them with a toolbox from which they can utilize their own creativity to tackle a series of problems. To elaborate, the tools given to the player ought to interact with the game's core ruleset and the problems the player faces should be derived from that ruleset.

A recent paragon of this is *The Legend of Zelda: Breath of the Wild*. Here, players are quickly given a series of items and taught the basic rules of the game's world. The toolbox in *Breath of the Wild* is the physics system itself, while many of the problems players are given to solve are optional, the game world provides almost infinite opportunities to interact with the physics system in new and interesting ways. A basic example of this is the grass that occupies a very large percentage of the world map. When the player uses any fire item (of which there are many: fire swords, fire arrows, etc.) a small patch of grass will catch fire. This results in an updraft which the player may then jump into with their glider to gain higher altitude.

The rafts are more involved. Many lakes and rivers have a small raft along the shore to allow players to paddle at a rate faster than Link (the player character) can swim. These rafts have a small sail attached to them to catch wind from the game's weather system. If the player kills octorok enemies, they are given a balloon-like item as loot. Creative players can tie a series of balloons to the raft, resulting in it hovering. Players can then use Link's leaf item to propel their makeshift airship.

A word of warning though: providing players with a set of tools allows player freedom and experimentation that can lead players to find unintended solutions to some game challenges. For example, the Lost Woods area is a forest containing a desirable item. In an effort to make the item relatively difficult to obtain, the Lost Woods are designed as a sort of maze without walls. When players enter the forest they are greeted with many trees and a thick fog. They must navigate the Lost Woods carefully by following the music and subtle lighting cues to guide them to the item. A wrong turn results in immediate teleportation back to the forest entrance. However, players have used the game's toolset to forgo navigation of the maze entirely. Across the river from the Lost Woods is a hill on top of which lies a large boulder. Players discovered they could use the Stasis ability on the boulder and freeze its momentum. If they then hit it multiple times with powerful weapons and quickly get on top of the boulder before it unfreezes, the boulder and the player are catapulted forward at an extremely high velocity over the magic fog of the Lost Woods and safely to the item's location in the center of the forest.

Such a design allows players to use their creativity, while also challenging their critical thinking skills. This results in the players feeling the same sense of accomplishment that a well-executed puzzle would promote. Additionally, players can solve problems in a myriad of ways, thereby extending the replayability of the game.

Unique and Challenging Achievements can Provide Players with Motivation to Re-Visit Old Content

LEE NEUSCHWANDER

If you've played any game in recent years, you're probably familiar with achievement systems: a meta-goal that exists outside of a particular game, but rewards and recognizes something done inside a game. But, did you ever think about what purpose these achievements serve in terms of game design? Sometimes, achievements are used to highlight specific challenges that require playing a game in a way that normally might not be attempted. These might include performing some crazy action or beating an enemy in a creative way.

These achievements encourage players to perform actions in the game that they would normally never attempt, while also informing them of additional gameplay possibilities they might not have considered. Players that succeed at these will take pride in their achievement. For example, *Team Fortress 2* (TF2) has an achievement called *Master of Disguise* that requires the player to trick an enemy support player into healing them while playing as a disguised spy. In addition to the feeling of superiority for a con well executed, players learn that disguised spies should behave like regular players on the team they are impersonating!

Now, for some veterans of the game this task may seem trivial, but achievements like these give players a specific task and reason to play the game in, possibly, a different way than they've been playing thus far. In this way, the game has coaxed the player to expand the ways that they had previously played the game. The same can be said for just about any of *World of Warcraft*'s dungeon achievements, in how they ask the player to perform a specific task in a dungeon that, although it makes the dungeon slightly more difficult, provides the player with a fresh perspective on old content.

So, to make the connection clear, achievements can be used as a great way to get players to, in a sense, do everything in the game. This could include going to an area they might not usually visit, performing an action that they would normally never do, or even just to provide a view of the game that is fresh and or otherwise new within the setting of old content.

Original snack idea by Aaron Low.

Let Your Players Customize Their Own Risk/Reward Ratios

KENDAL KOTTER

Many games come equipped with a variety of difficulty settings, ranging from story-only modes to "I'm-a-glutton-for-punishment" modes. While these modes are great for generally influencing the difficulty of the game, they aren't customized to a player's individual strengths and weaknesses. This can leave players in situations where certain modes are too hard in some areas, but not hard enough in others. For example, perhaps a player excels in combat against melee enemies, but struggles when up against ranged opponents. Increasing the difficulty level will, as a whole, grant the player appropriately challenging combat when up against melee enemies, but will further punish their weakness against ranged enemies. This one-size-fits-all approach can result in lackluster gaming experiences and a disappointed player. To solve this issue, consider exploring player-customizable difficulty settings that are individualized to certain subsets of combat, exploration or other gameplay-centric areas.

Giving players control over their own risk/reward ratio allows each individual player to create a gameplay situation where they feel appropriately challenged – and can change it as soon as they feel the challenge is no longer appropriate. This is a somewhat similar approach to adding collectibles into your game, but whereas collectibles are built outside of the story (and are often collected through post-game playthroughs), smaller-scoped difficulty customization is intended to be used on the first play through, and then any subsequent playthroughs. This allows players to play at their optimal difficulty on a level by level basis, instead of making a single decision that then affects the entire game.

This is used to great effect in Supergiant's *Bastion*. Early in the game, players are given access to what are called idols. These idols give players access to modular difficulty settings, allowing them to select the specific areas of the game that they'd like to play at a higher difficulty level. Players can customize the idols they have equipped before entering any level. Idols can have effects such as increasing enemy health regeneration, slowing player movement speed after attacking, or increasing enemy attack damage. The more idols equipped, the higher the difficulty, but also the higher the rewards. Equipping idols increases experience gain percentages for the player, thus incentivizing players to make use of the idols consistently. All of this combines to grant players a greater sense of freedom and choice in their gameplay experience.

Allowing players to customize their gameplay difficulty at a more granular level instead of a game-wide level hands more control back to the players. Two other examples of games that use this type of difficulty system are *Pyre* and *Celeste*.

Original snack idea by Nicholas Stewart.

VARIETY IN GAMEPLAY

What do game designers do to provide more gameplay options?

Randomized Character Names and Traits Can Lead to More Engaging Experiences

LEE NEUSCHWANDER

You're playing an RPG and stumble across a village. Which seems more interesting: talking to "Local Weapon Shopkeeper" or "Dan Blackthumb"? The answer is pretty obvious: an NPC with a name goes a lot further than one with a generic name, or even no name at all. Names hint at stories, and often all that is needed is the hint of a story for players to get more interested or curious about the characters in a game. You don't have to create the backstory for good old Blackthumb and friends. Players will take it upon themselves to fill in the blanks when given enough tidbits of information to work with – perhaps another character in the village has the same last name, are they related? Is there a story behind the unusual surname? Maybe another villager has clues – "Oh, we don't like to talk about the incident anymore".

A few seeds of information that can be randomly distributed around characters that would otherwise be nameless and generic, can help create a play experience that feels personal and interesting. The randomization can end up contributing to the player's sense of ownership and connection to the world and the game – their friend's shopkeeper might be "Jacob Baldrump" with different implied backstories based on different random nuggets of information.

Randomizing character-related elements even works for player characters! In *Rogue Legacy*, players control a randomly generated character who has a unique name, appearance, abilities, and traits. These randomized abilities affect the game in meaningful ways. The player then has to make the best of that character during their playthrough. When the character dies, a portrait is added to the game's "family tree" and the player must then select their next character: the heir to the previous one. By keeping track of prior characters, and due to the randomization of their names and traits, each player creates their own unique family history in a way that feels engaging and satisfying. Each character becomes an extension of the player and the family tree gives real impact and proof of the player affecting the game world. What makes *Rogue Legacy* stand out is how randomized characters and other in-game elements have been incorporated to give each player a story that is both unique to their playthrough, and builds on the story of all their playthroughs.

The heir system where each generation gets randomized traits (Rogue Legacy).

Careful Repetition of Challenges Allows for Novel but Familiar Player Experiences

TREVOR SCOTT RICHARD

A good video-game level, like a good account of history, is more than just "one damn thing after another". Skilled designers are able to craft sequences that are more than the sum of their parts by meticulously arranging various enemies and obstacles in a particular order. Although the subtle intentionality of such efforts might not be immediately apparent on a player's first playthrough of a game, careful analysis can reveal a number of tricks designers use to make their levels feel more cohesive. One of the most common of these methods is to gradually escalate a particular challenge by repeating different versions of it multiple times within the same level.

There are many variations of this technique. Generally speaking, a new challenge is introduced in a relatively safe environment, expanded upon throughout the course of the level, and finally presented in its most difficult or impressive form. 2D platformers tend to demonstrate the efficacy of this pattern particularly well, and Matt Makes Games' *Celeste* is no exception. Its "Golden Ridge" level, for example, includes powerful winds which affect Madeline's ability to jump. The first screen to feature wind consists of little more than a few generously positioned platforms, offering the player a chance to learn how the wind works independent of other variables. Throughout the level, the speed of the wind increases and the screens on which it appears become more dangerous, culminating in a gauntlet of ferociously fast gales and treacherously tiny platforms. Although this final challenge is certainly difficult, it remains approachable due to the opportunity the player has been given to explore the level's central ideas in gradually more complex situations.

Another advantage of levels which progress in this manner is that they allow designers to layer challenges on top of each other in interesting ways. The final chapter of *Celeste*'s main story remixes ideas from all of its previous chapters into one last, laborious climb to the top of the mountain. Without proper presentation of its mechanics, this penultimate section could have been confusing and rage-inducing. However, since the game allows the player to develop a deep understanding of its various components throughout their playthrough, the last level is instead a masterpiece of momentous and well-paced design, full of intricately arranged obstacles for the player to overcome. One screen features wind which, rather than pushing against Madeline, blows at her back and increases the horizontal velocity of her jump. This sudden increase in speed layers a demand for faster reactions on top of the level's maze of spikes, making safe navigation even more dangerous than usual. Again, although this screen (and the level as a whole) is tough, the player's determination to conquer all challenges that lay before them is buoyed by the knowledge and confidence they've gained throughout the course of the game, thanks to its deliberate escalation of similar mechanical ideas. In other words, there isn't anything new – but the arrangement of elements makes for a novel challenge that is still familiar.

This approach to level design works just as well in games that aren't as masochistically challenging as *Celeste*. The 2018 version of *Spider-Man* does this with its combat system. Players are slowly introduced to new moves at the same time that new enemies appear, against whom those moves are particularly effective. By the end of the game, the player has a huge variety of moves that can be combined to result in amazing action sequences that resemble and even surpass those seen in the comics and movies.

Be sure to look for more examples of this technique in action, and also watch for it in other types of games. Good level design is good level design, regardless of genre.

Repairable Weapon Degradation Encourages Weapon Use and Reduces Hoarding

LEE NEUSCHWANDER

Some games have systems in which weapons and/or items degrade over time as they are used by players until they are ultimately destroyed or rendered useless. What are some of the effects of including this design feature? Players might appreciate the greater realism, strategizing on how and when to use certain items becomes a concern, and there is often some frustration upon losing items when/if they break. Players feel that losing their weapons through use is akin to the game robbing them of the rewards that they work hard to achieve. This can be especially frustrating when you lose a nice weapon against some low-level enemies. That's like using a full health restore potion after taking only one point of damage. It's wasteful, pointless and in the end, makes the player feel horrible about making a clear mistake. That's no fun at all.

Perhaps the most negative effect is that players might stop using rare, or otherwise special items entirely – keeping them for that moment when they will be needed to save the day. Strangely, this moment never comes and players end up behaving like hoarders, carrying around all kinds of nice loot but never using it because, "What if I need it later on when I get to a really hard monster?"

One solution is to vary the availability of the items/weapons – if players perceive them as less rare or special, perhaps they won't fret about using them in the first place. If you're holding on to two Swords of Lightning, you're more likely to use one while saving the other one as "backup". But, that results in rare and special items feeling, well, less special and exciting.

The Witcher 3 and *World of Warcraft* both have degradation of weapons and armor. However, they remove the fear of permanently losing an item by allowing players to restore the usefulness of the item by repairing it for a maintenance cost. This clever addition means that players can enjoy the strategic decisions that come from deciding what to use and when, while keeping the sense of reward from finding/earning a powerful new weapon to aid them in their adventures. Of course, it is still important to make sure that the rate of degradation is just right: weapons that break after two swings result in heroes feeling less like adventurers and more like suckers of the fantasy military-industrial complex. On the other hand, if a player can go through multiple major encounters without having to worry about their gear degrading, why bother including that game system in the first place?

How to Do Drastic Gameplay Changes the Right Way

KENDAL KOTTER

"Water levels". Every platformer seems to have them, and yet players seem to universally regard them with at least trepidation, if not disgust. "Water levels" can be problematic, in large part because they indicate a radical shift in gameplay: controls change, mechanics you could previously use are now either missing or drastically different, and learned game skills and knowledge either don't apply or are detrimental. The flow of the game is interrupted, and if not done correctly, can be viewed as frustrating, out-of-place, and poorly designed. But not all radical gameplay shifts (and water levels) are bad.

So, how can such radical shifts in gameplay be done right? What works in one game could fail miserably in another. However, here are some things to consider when designing gameplay shifts:

Is the gameplay shift narratively justified? Gameplay shifts should be wholeheartedly supported by the in-game narrative. If the gameplay shift is radical, there should be some sort of significant event or reason in the narrative to support that shift. For example, in *Uncharted: Drake's Fortune*, the players must suddenly face a new kind of enemy that is quite different from everything they've encountered previously: the shift in tone is both foreshadowed by the game's narrative so far, but also ultimately explained – it's an airborne virus that has infected its victims, turning them feral and zombie-like.

Does the gameplay shift require re-learning the controls and gameplay? Players will get frustrated quickly if the radical gameplay is completely out of the realm of the rest of the game. At their best, gameplay shifts should feel like creative innovations of current mechanics, not additions of completely unrelated mechanics.

Is it appropriately difficult? Such a sudden change in gameplay may require the radically different areas of the game to be tuned down difficulty-wise in order to avoid player frustration. Platformer *Rayman Legends* features "music levels" with sudden gameplay changes – there are no puzzles, they're fast and tense, and players lose the freedom of exploration they normally have. However, their core gameplay is in many ways less demanding – players mostly jump and attack only – but they must generally do so in time with the music. While these levels are not "easy" – the shift in gameplay works because the player needs to concentrate on fewer things and is supported by the music.

Finally, does the radical gameplay shift add anything to the game? Is it an improvement to the game and the player's experience with it? Radical gameplay shifts can be exciting for players. As a designer, just make sure that the shifts are included in a way that adds to the game instead of inadvertently taking away from it.

Non-Violent Ways of Resolving Conflicts Makes Games More Interesting for Players

JACOB GRAHMANN

Many games feature shooting, stabbing, punching, kicking and other fighting as their primary mechanic. More attention should be given to games that focus on resolving conflict outside of physical intervention, because games that offer non-violent conflict resolution present more interesting choices to the player. Games designed around mechanics that don't require the player to kill anything to progress challenge conventions and norms and provide unexpected gameplay.

Undertale is a popular indie game that implements this well. The game is renowned, partly because of its combat system that allows players to pacify or subdue monsters rather than kill them. The choices made by players in combat also have an effect on the dialogue and story as players make progress. The pacifist route introduces new gameplay that's harder than the violent route, forcing players to make difficult decisions. As mentioned, this has all sorts of narrative implications, but more relevantly, it also affects the gameplay in an interesting way; players are now encouraged to think about how to appeal to their opponent as a nuanced character.

Allowing players to resolve conflicts in various ways presents players with new perspectives and decisions not normally found in traditional games. *Middle Earth: Shadow of War* does this by allowing you to convert enemy captains and warchiefs to your side to fight as your captains and commanding officers. Even though pursuing this route is more difficult, it strengthens the player's army and allows them to defend their territories more easily. Allowing players to have alternatives to resolve conflict provides the means for players to express themselves through the character in a way that they see fit.

Implementing mechanics that allow players to resolve conflicts in multiple ways encourages player expression, in that players can interact with the world in a way that they see either through themselves or their character. Multiple ways to resolve conflict resolution could lead to multiple path's the player could take to complete the game. This encourages diverse gameplay experiences over multiple playthroughs, along with increasing game replayability. It's also more realistic – after all, we mostly resolve problems and issues in our lives without resorting to violence.

Original snack idea by Trevor Scott Richard.

Being Overpowered Can Help Players Better Understand a Game

KENDAL KOTTER

Overpowered (OP) weapons in games are a common occurrence, and for good reason. It's a satisfying experience to use weapons, abilities or other mechanics that are drastically more effective than what a player is used to. However, if these overpowered items are not doled out to the player with some moderation, they quickly lose their value, and transition into becoming a game design problem. In these cases, allowing players to be over-powered can be a terrible idea.

That being said, there are at least a few effective ways of incorporating overpowered items and abilities into a game. Many games start the player with a character that has fully-leveled abilities and high-damage items. This situation allows a player to experience endgame potential while being able to learn the game in a safe environment (the player is sufficiently overpowered that nothing can harm them). This situation gives players a taste of power, hooking them immediately into the gameplay and encouraging them to continue playing past the overpowered section. *Metroid Prime* does this effectively, starting the player off with all of the character's equipment and upgrades. Shortly after making it through the tutorial section and defeating the boss, however, the player's character is damaged and all of the equipment is lost. Losing powers and abilities is not generally fun: players don't like the feeling of losing something they were enjoying. Fortunately, there is another way to allow players to experience being OP without breaking the game.

Breath of Fire IV allows players to periodically play as the game's main villain, who is ridiculously overpowered. Players are given a glimpse of the game's potential power in a limited time environment, which encourages them to continue playing the game (as well as making later fights against the villain more tense and exciting). Playing as the villain for a while is a great way for players to better understand the motivations of the baddie, but it's also a way for them to know, first hand, how tough things will be in the end, and have something exciting to look forward to in the final showdown! If the villain has special abilities, players can also learn what they do as they use them, and – if they're clever – begin to formulate strategies they can use later against the villain.

Allowing players to experience carefully designed moments of excessive power can be beneficial. It grants players an opportunity to temporarily relieve gameplay stress, learn new mechanics without fear of failure, and provide tantalizing glimpses of future content – and it's fun to boot.

Original snack idea by Yuqi Shi.

USER INTERFACE AND VISUAL INFORMATION

What can game designers do to more effectively present information to their players?

The User Interface Can Help the Player Share in their Character's Experience

LEE NEUSCHWANDER

One of the main goals of a good user interface (UI) is to provide relevant information to the player in a way that is clear and efficient. There are all kinds of information that need to be presented. This can include information on the general state of things, like the player's current score, or how many lives they have left. The UI also shows information that might be necessary to play the game effectively, such as button prompts on the screen telling the player what to press next or what to do. However, the UI should also help the player to better connect with the game's characters.

Consider the case of game dialogue. In many games, dialogue is presented to the player as text inside a rectangular window. There is often also a static picture of the character speaking. The shape of the window and the design of its frame can be altered to, for example, show that the character speaking is scared or angry. This is similar to how the shape of speech bubbles in comic books indicates the tone and emotion of something that was said. If the bubble (or text window, in games) is "spiky" then its content was shouted and there is anger or excitement in the speaker's voice. In games, the character's picture is also changed to reflect this. These two design elements can help players to better connect with the characters. But, it's not really enough. Just because a character says something in a scared voice, and their image looks afraid, doesn't mean that the player will also feel scared.

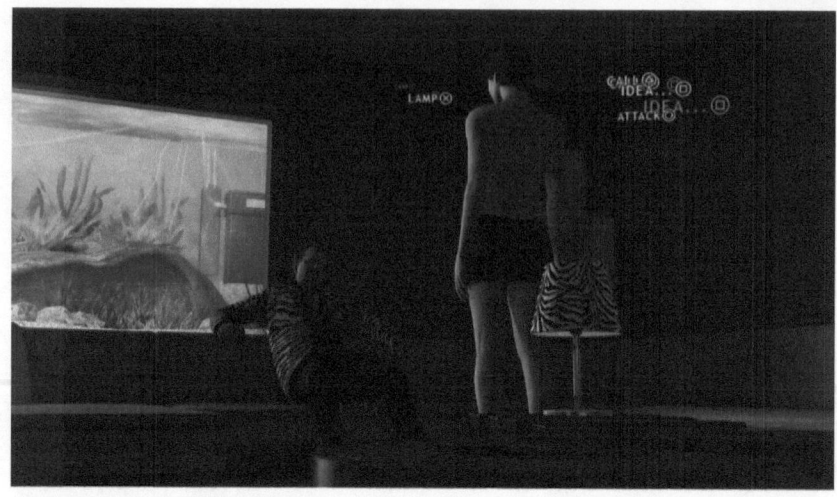

Floating icons that indicate actions as well as in-world locations of those actions (Heavy Rain) (Image source: dailymotion.com)

Heavy Rain helps players feel closer to what the game's characters may be experiencing by making changes to the way the UI works. The game displays floating icons indicating what the player must do with their controller to interact with things in the gameworld (press a button, move a thumbstick in an upward direction, etc.). Other times there might be a few floating icons indicating a choice the character needs to make. However, when the character is stressed out, or in a really intense situation, the floating icons move around the screen erratically. This reflects how it feels to be the character at that moment: stressed and pressured in such that they cannot calmly reflect on what to do next. When coupled with audio and controller vibrations this creates a complex and exciting way to get the player to really feel engaged with the character they are controlling. In this case, when the character is in a state such that they cannot calmly make a decision, this emotional experience is passed along to the player. The erratic movement of the icons also makes it hard to understand what the options are and, especially when there is a time limit or other external pressure (like a threatening antagonist!), the player might just make the kind of poor snap judgment the character would realistically do in that situation. Through the UI, a nervous and jumpy character can also result in a nervous and jumpy player!

Diegetic UI Helps the Player Care More About the Gameworld and its Characters

BENJAMIN BARKER

Some games use diegetic UI to encourage players to better connect with, and care about, the game's world and its characters.

Diegetic UI refers to user interface elements that actually exist within the game world. So, in a first-person shooter, a counter on the side of the screen indicating how many bullets are left in a magazine would be diegetic. An ammunition icon in the corner of the screen displaying the same information would not.

In *Firewatch*, players control a rookie fire lookout in the Shoshone National Forest in Wyoming. Exploring is a large portion of the game. Players commonly get lost in these kinds of games. To avoid this, the UI often includes some sort of map, icons and waypoints to help players orient themselves. *Firewatch*, however, only provides the character with a compass and a paper map. There are no waypoints or floating icons in either the world or map. The player must hold out the compass and determine their direction using the map and nearby landmarks. Furthermore, when the player is looking at the map, it is held up, obscuring the character's view. In this way, the player feels much more connected to the character and the events in the game – the player feels disoriented and lost (like the character), and over time learns how to navigate their surroundings (again, like the character).

Hellblade: Senua's Sacrifice is an action game in which the player controls Senua, a Pict woman with psychosis who is on a quest to save the soul of her lost love. *Hellblade*'s UI has two important diegetic elements: Senua's arm rot and the voices in her head. When Senua dies, a black rot grows farther and farther up her arm. The player is told in no uncertain terms that if the rot ever reaches Senua's head, the game will end and all their saved data will be erased. This threat is constantly in the player's vision, a reminder that not only keeps the player immersed, but one which continually underlines the anxiety Senua feels, causing the player to feel the same, thus empathizing with her immensely. As for the voices in Senua's head, while some are antagonistic, others are helpful and will shout out at the player in dire times informing them if their health is low, or if there are enemies behind them. Just as the arm rot serves to heighten the tension by translating Senua's experience onto the player, these voices likewise serve to put the player in Senua's position. These two systems combine to create an emotionally harrowing and deeply immersive player experience.

The rot on Senua's arm, reminding the player of their failures (Hellblade: Senua's Sacrifice)

When the UI is integrated into the game world it helps keep the player immersed. If, for example, a player is running low on ammo, and the character's model reflects this in some way, the player is not pulled out of the moment to check the status of such a valuable resource. This not only keeps the players actively engaged in gameplay, but also increases the pathos they feel for their character. When a character's immediate vicinity contains valuable information, the player will look at the model more often in a gameplay session and, due to the ever-changing state of a given resource, the character will feel much more alive.

Original snack idea by Kendall Kotter.

Camera Perspectives Show/ Obscure Info that Allow for Different Gameplay Challenges

TREVOR SCOTT RICHARD

Camera perspective is an important game design choice. Whether a game takes place in first-person or third-person, 2D or 3D, etc., has a significant impact on how it plays. This aspect of game design often goes unnoticed, partly because some video-game genres seem synonymous with the perspective they typically employ (say, first-person shooters). Nonetheless, there are a number of games we can look to for examples of how various camera perspectives affect challenges in gameplay.

Perhaps the best place to start is the mid-90s, when console games were first making the jump from 2D to 3D. Consider how this change in perspective affected the *Legend of Zelda* games. Early entries in the series, like *A Link to the Past* (ALttP), feature labyrinthic dungeons which require the player to exercise nonlinear spatial reasoning. While ALttP's top-down perspective affords players enough simultaneous architectural information to make this a reasonable task, it turns out to be much more complicated in the series' 3D endeavors because their ground-level perspective makes this architectural information less immediately apprehensible. To compensate, the dungeons in *Ocarina of Time* (OoT) are significantly less structurally complex than those of its predecessors. However, because OoT and other 3D Zelda titles feature a more realistically dimensional camera perspective, they can confront players with problems that simply would not be approachable in 2D. Take the Snowhead dungeon in *Majora's Mask*. While the high-level structure of this dungeon is fairly linear and straightforward, successfully navigating it is challenging due to its main feature: a massive pillar in its center which blocks entry to rooms on various floors. To make progress, players must selectively reposition this pillar in order to access these rooms in the correct order. Doing this requires them to think about the dungeon as a genuine 3D space, which would be difficult to convey accurately in a 2D game. The key insight here is that camera perspective affects gameplay by affecting the visual information available to the player.

Crash Bandicoot also exemplifies the effect of camera perspective on information availability – for better or worse. Interestingly, the camera perspective frequently changes between levels. While some of the game's levels are effectively two-dimensional (progress is made entirely by moving left to right, or vice versa), others are more apparently three-dimensional in that they require Crash to make progress by running toward or away from the camera. Levels in which Crash runs toward the camera are uniquely treacherous in that anticipating obstacles becomes more difficult than usual. This challenge, as with those of other levels in *Crash Bandicoot*, is directly related to the camera perspective being employed and how that perspective highlights or obscures certain types of information.

The effect of camera perspective on information availability can be seen in virtually any video-game. It's often easier to see nearby enemies in games like *Uncharted* or *Gears of War* than in games like *Call of Duty* or *Battlefield*, because the third-person view tends to grant a wider field of view than the first-person. For further examples, take a game and ask yourself some questions about its use of perspective: How would this game play if it were 2D instead of 3D, or vice-versa? What would change about this game if it were first-person, third-person, etc.? The more you start to think about this aspect of game design, the more connections you'll be able to draw between how a game looks and how it plays.

Original snack idea by Nicholas Stewart.

Fog of War Can Add to the Immersive Experience of a Game

JACOB GRAHMANN

In many strategy games, locations of enemies or resources on the map or level are hidden from the player unless they have a unit or character that can "see" them. This is called the fog of war (FoW), which we can think of as sort of anti-UI. Fog of war is used to create uncertainty and also affect the intended style of play – for example, it makes it important for players to explore and "see" the gameworld in order to get strategic information. It can also be used to pace player's progression: forcing players to play more conservatively and second-guess themselves as they consider their options (and what their opponent might be doing).

Door Kickers is a tactical strategy game where the player controls a police squad that must move through buildings during raids, or deal with hostage situations against terrorists and criminals. During missions, the player can only see a basic layout of the building and everything within the line of sight of their officers. Using FoW really puts the players in the shoes of the officers: you know the general overview of the situation you must respond to, but you are going in almost blind. Before starting the level you're given an estimate of how many enemies your officers might face, then the game randomizes the enemy's actual numbers and locations.

It is crucial for players to carefully plan how their officers enter rooms and move through hallways. If players fail to tell their officers to check the corners or small rooms they walk by, the fog of war will conceal hidden enemies, and their officer will be injured or killed. This forces the player to plan their routes carefully and slowly, because once an officer is killed in action, they are permanently removed from your squad and valuable experience is lost. The FoW during these levels creates emotional tension within the player. Over multiple levels, players can create attachments to squad members as they are promoted and gain skill. Knowing the consequences of what could happen if the player instructs the officers poorly creates a sense of duty within the player to keep their squad safe, reinforcing the theme of the game.

If this game were to remove its fog of war mechanic, it would be much less enjoyable and less emotionally gripping. By using the fog of war mechanic, *Door Kickers* offers players unique, immersive gameplay experiences through level randomization and uncertainty in tense situations.

Drawing Attention to Important Information in Multiple Ways Helps Players Understand Faster

MCKENNA CALDWELL

A health meter is something most players are familiar with. Sometimes it is a few hearts in the corner of the screen that disappear as the player takes a hit. Or maybe it is a filled bar that depletes when the player is losing health. Just as players are familiar with the concept of health and its depletion, players are also familiar with being so engrossed in the actions they are performing they forget to notice their health meter is dropping. Suddenly, the game is over and the player realizes they just forgot to look at their current health.

The health meter is a little different in *Infamous 2*. When Cole MacGrath's health is dropping, the color starts to drain from the screen, the music slows, and bloody-colored splotches overlay the screen. It's difficult to miss, and the effects increase over time, giving the player a sense of how low their health is. Then, as a player drains electricity from the world to heal Cole, the music speeds up quickly, the color returns, and the gore clears from the screen. The game notifies the player both visually and audibly when they need to heal. Cole's health feels more real for the player, giving a feeling of sluggishness and exhaustion as the music slows its frantic pace and the world loses color.

Giving the player the information they need in both a visual and audible way helps emphasize it so that it cannot be missed. It is harder for players to ask, "What just happened?" when the game was yelling and waving the explanation at them. This technique can be applied in different ways. Perhaps, instead of an ammunition count, a firing gun sounds different when it is running out of ammo. Enemies might stagger and bleed to show their health, in addition to the bar above their heads. These techniques can also contribute to the game's world feeling more natural and immersive, instead of technical and overlaid.

When a player loses health the screen changes to black and white with blood splatter around the edges of the screen, and it becomes hard to see (Infamous 2)

In *Super Mario Sunshine*, Mario uses a water pump to clean up polluted enemies and the mess they leave behind. The pump's water storage is represented by a meter on the screen that depletes as Mario uses water. The pump also squeaks audibly and changes the way it sounds as it runs out. This tells the player they need to refill in two helpful ways, instead of only one, so that the information is relayed quickly and easily to the player.

It's said that information is power, and this is certainly true in games. If a player knows more information about characters and the game world, they will be able to have more fun playing and play better. Players rely on a game's sound and visuals to give them the information they need to play the game. As designers, we should strive to make sound and visuals that tell the player what they need to know in ways that feel natural and match the style of the game. We should make it as easy as possible for the player to have the power they need to play our games.

Original snack idea by Shakti Das.

MULTI-PURPOSE DESIGN

How do game designers get multiple uses from design elements?

It is Often Better to Use One Button for Many Things

TREVOR SCOTT RICHARD

The PlayStation 4 controller boasts four traditional buttons, four shoulder buttons, a four-way D-pad, two joysticks, a pseudo-touchpad, and three menu buttons; the NES controller featured exactly four buttons (including Start and Select) and a four-way D-pad. Clearly, more controls mean more sophisticated gameplay, no? After all, fewer physical inputs mean fewer actions a player character could perform as the result of a single button press. This might be true sometimes, but not always!

Clever design allows for a single button to do multiple things, thus providing a richer gameplay experience for the player, while making the game more approachable – no need to require a player use all the buttons on a controller, while remembering what each of them does. Nintendo's flagship hero, Mario, is the unavoidable poster-child for this design approach. Ever since his debut in the early 80s, this portly plumber has offered players an ever increasing variety of gameplay experiences, almost always centered on jumping. In the original *Super Mario Bros*, the player dodges obstacles, attacks enemies, grabs power-ups, and more, all with just two main buttons: run and jump. Even in later titles with more mechanics, Mario games tended to revolve around one or two central ideas. In *Super Mario Sunshine*, the player accomplishes tasks primarily with Mario's water-jetpack, and *Super Mario Odyssey* allows the player to interact with virtually everything in the game by throwing Mario's hat. By centering their games on just a few ideas and putting those ideas to as many uses as possible, Nintendo is able to create games that are easy to understand and simple to control, and can be enjoyed thoroughly by players of all skill levels. In the words of Mario's creator, Shigeru Miyamoto, "A great idea solves multiple problems at the same time". In this case, the same button does different things depending on the context – where the player is located as well as what they've just done.

Overloading buttons in this way can sometimes be a problem. For example, if pressing "X" results in a door opening, or picking up an item, designers shouldn't leave items next to doors. But, when done well – that is avoiding problems where players wanted to perform one action, but did another instead – assigning multiple actions to the same input is a great way to reduce complexity. Fewer buttons to press and richer options for players!

As video-game hardware has improved and controllers have acquired more and more buttons, many games continue to employ ideas which solve multiple problems in the service of elegant design. The arm cannon in *Metroid* is used both to defeat enemies and open doors; *Minecraft* players employ the same basic toolset to gather resources, craft items, and fight monsters; and *Fortnite*'s crafting mechanics are useful for both navigation and combat. Even series' like *Street Fighter* and *Mortal Kombat* demonstrate the utility of this approach when they pack their games with more moves than could ever be individually mapped to a controller's inputs, by making use of intricate button combos, which results in each button's necessity to multiple moves. As you continue your journey into the world of video-game design, keep an eye out for instances where designers have managed to kill two (or more!) birds with one stone, and another eye out for missed opportunities to do so.

Original snack idea by Jinrui Hu.

Quick Time Events can be used to Build Tension and/or Empower Players

JACOB GRAHMANN

Quick time events (QTE), when done well can leave the player feeling mighty and in control of their character; done poorly, they can break the players sense of immersion. QTEs are a situational tool that prompts players to input an action on the controller shortly after a command is given on-screen. They are generally used during cutscenes and visual sequences within a game, and accomplish two things: allow characters to perform complex actions beyond the standard control scheme, and engage players during otherwise non-interactive visual sequences. Performing the wrong input during a QTE generally results in game changing consequences, loss of player health, or a game over. Games that implement QTEs well try to avoid repetitive actions that can break their immersion by causing the task required of them to feel predictable. More broadly however, QTEs can be used to surprise players and keep the game's experience fresh and exciting.

In the *God of War* series, quick-time events are often utilized as finishing moves against bosses. This allows players to participate in Kratos' performance of epic, complex actions that are consistent with Kratos' character, but are otherwise impossible to achieve with the standard control scheme. Unique bosses call for unique, surprising and exciting QTE boss take-downs. Through the use of QTEs, players get to feel powerful since they have a greater sense of control over the character who is doing unique and varied things in the game environment.

In the survival horror game *Until Dawn*, the player generally has reduced control over the individual actions of the characters. Instead, players spend a fair amount of time watching the characters as the story progresses. As the story unfolds, the developers implemented quick-time events during moments of the game when player mistakes could be story changing. The decisions of the players during these QTE's can decide which characters live or whether you can complete the game with a happy ending. By implementing QTE's in this way, the developers successfully added some player agency to an otherwise narrative-heavy game. The players decisions and reactions are vital to the outcome of the game and, they also capture the attention of players during other longer, non-interactive sequences. Some of these moments are tense and dramatic – and the limiting control that the QTE's give creates a sense of panic in players that really complements the game's horror theme.

QTEs can surprise players in good ways by showing them novel and exciting gameplay moments like Krato's special killer moves, and by reinforcing the mood of a horror game like in *Until Dawn*. It is always important that QTEs feel fresh and novel; there is little worse that when a player can predict the QTE ahead of time or maybe even worse – have to play the same one too many times in a row! Due to many games using bad QTE's, players are sometimes skeptical of games that include them. This is why, when considering the use of QTE's in a game, much thought should be given to how it adds to the gameplay instead of limiting it, but more importantly, how does it add to the game's experience?

Original snack idea by Jinrui Hu.

In-Game Collectables Should Have Purpose and Build Upon the Game

MCKENNA CALDWELL

When collectables are well designed, they can encourage exploration, build lore and story, give rewards, and be fun for players to seek out. Collectibles should always strive to be optional, appropriate in number, easy or enjoyable to retrieve, and give the player some type of reward.

Horizon Zero Dawn does all the right things with its collectibles. There are four types of collectibles the player can seek out in the game's beautiful open world. Vantage Points are special locations that, when discovered by the player, communicate a small bit of lore and worldbuilding story. Ancient Vessels, Metal Flowers, and Banuk Artifacts are special items that when found can be sold to different merchants for weapon upgrades and in-game currency. While players can purchase special maps that mark the locations of these collectibles, the game design does a terrific job of guiding players to each area the collectibles can be found in. This makes it easy for a player to simply play the game, finding and collecting items along the way. This can be pleasing for players whose goal is to reach 100% game completion and for players that just want to casually play through the game.

Poorly designed collectibles can be a frustrating addition to any game when there are too many and they give no reward. Some games have collectibles that serve no real purpose and feel as if they were only added to make the game seem larger. A bad collectible system can sometimes cause player burnout, making them feel bored with the game overall, or frustrate players by making the game feel artificially full of things that don't provide actual substance to the game.

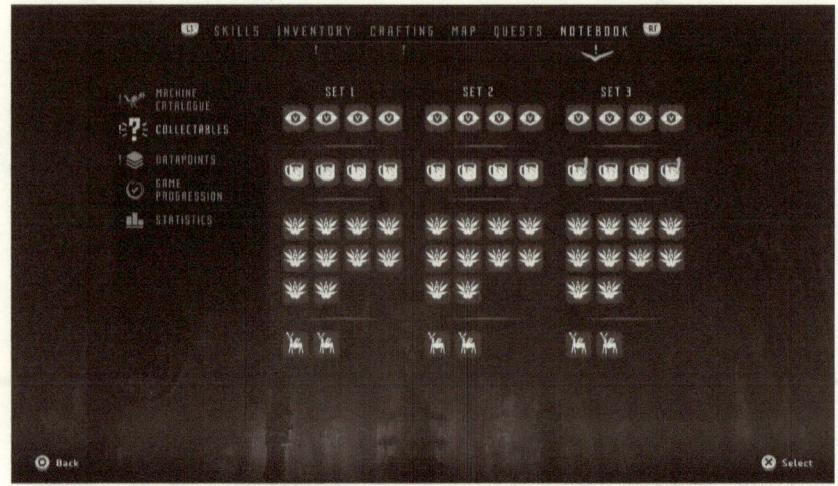

List of Collectibles (Horizon Zero Dawn)

In *Spider-Man* there are six different types of tokens. Tokens serve as a form of in-game currency that can be used to craft suits, gadgets and mods to help the player in combat and world traversal. Each token type is earned in a different way. Some, like Crime Tokens, require the player to seek out and thwart acts of crime across Manhattan, and reward players with additional tokens for completing combat in specific ways. Backpack Tokens require the player to find Peter Parker's old backpacks left throughout the city. Backpacks also provide a bit of backstory as Peter describes the contents, telling stories of past events or detailing his relationships with other characters. The amazingly, fun way in which Spider-Man traverses the world makes collecting these items both enjoyable and rewarding. Another collectible in the game are 12 pigeons that must be found and then caught. It's the only collectible set that doesn't reward the player with anything more than a thank you from a grateful citizen. But catching the birds uses the mechanics very well, and it feels so perfectly in character to catch them all, that it doesn't become a chore.

Reward Systems that Unite Gameplay and Story Support Immersive Feedback Loops

TREVOR SCOTT RICHARD

Due to the interactive nature of the medium, video-games afford their creators the opportunity to tell stories in a manner that is utterly unique. Games that take full advantage of this opportunity often stand out as unusually memorable, while those that squander it risk fragmenting their core experience. One way to avoid this fate and ensure that a game feels narratively and mechanically cohesive is to tie its story and gameplay together into the same reward system.

This approach is common in many games that focus on role-playing or exploratory immersion. Rather than primarily exposit plot through pre-rendered cutscenes, From Software's *Bloodborne*, for example, rewards its players for defeating enemies by providing them with narratively rich items. Each item's in-menu description offers both practical information and scattered bits of lore; consequently, learning about the game's story follows naturally from playing it. In similar fashion, Bethesda's *Skyrim* encourages exploration by leading players to NPCs and even virtual books from which they can learn about the history of the game's world, as well as by tempting them with the usual loot drops. By including narrative and mechanical rewards alongside one another, these games and others like them combine gameplay and story into a single immersive experience unlike any other.

Thekla Inc's *The Witness* also performs this kind of ludic alchemy particularly well. Solving the game's puzzles grants the player access not only to additional puzzles, but also to various audio and video recordings which convey the game's thematic ideas. Along with metaphorically reinforcing *The Witness'* mechanical themes, these recordings sometimes reveal additional hidden puzzles to the player. This creates a subtle feedback loop in which players progress through the game's world by uncovering its various narrative elements, which in turn occurs as they make progress through each new area – it's all wheels within wheels.

Even if 50-hour RPGs and obtuse puzzle adventures aren't your cup of tea, there's much to be said for ludonarratively harmonious reward systems. Whereas interruptive cutscenes might force a player to divide their focus between gameplay and story, any game that manages to seamlessly weld the two is likely to captivate its audience for hours at a time. Perhaps best of all, accomplishing such a feat via reward systems doesn't necessitate deferment to Hollywood tropes or any other sort of pretense to being 'more than a game'; all it requires it thoughtful world-building. Be sure to take note of the role this approach plays in enhancing your experience with whatever massive, story-driven game you dive into next – even if it does happen to be full of unskippable cutscenes.

PLAYING WITH OTHERS

What do game designers do to make playing with others more satisfying?

Letting your Players be Nice to Each Other can Reduce Toxicity

KENDAL KOTTER

In many cases, games that are ostensibly about teamwork become riddled with toxicity. This can be combated with systems that allow players on a team to reward and recognize their fellow teammates. This leads to successful multiplayer player experiences. Recognizing other players allows for a greater sense of camaraderie between teammates, promotes support and gratitude towards roles and players that might otherwise not receive it, and increases role diversity by highlighting the importance of lesser-seen roles and positions.

In many multiplayer games, the only information that players are granted about their peers' performance is the kill count and death count per player per match. When a game focuses solely on the kill and death count, players are encouraged to play in a style that results in a high number of kills. This pattern has slowly started to change, with a larger scope of information being available to the player: kill and death count, yes, but also such statistics as the amount of healing done, damage blocked with shields and armor, length of time that enemies are crowd-controlled, and more. With access to these stats, as well as games prompting players to honor others for significant success with these stats, games are encouraging players to step outside the only-damage-heavy roles.

In team-based games, where having a balance of roles on a team is essential, we see this pattern even more. Take *Overwatch*, for instance: at the end of every game, players can vote to congratulate players that the game identifies as having done exceptionally well. This allows players to recognize members of the team across all of the roles, whether that be the main damage dealer, or the support role that provided consistent and timely healing to the team. Players are more likely to play a variety of roles when they see the contributions that each role gives to the team as a whole.

League of Legends employs a similar end-of-game honor system, where players can honor fellow teammates in one of three categories: Stay Cool,

Great Shotcalling, and GG. These more generalized honors, devoid of any stats from the game that was just played, focus instead only on helping players recognize those teammates that contributed positively to their gaming experience. Systems like these help, at least marginally, to combat one of multiplayer gaming's biggest issues: toxicity. Many end-of-game honor voting systems, including the one in *Overwatch*, allow players to honor players on the opposing team. This encouragement of good sportsmanship is at least a small step forward into combating problems of abuse and harassment found within the multiplayer gaming community.

Offering players a way to honor and recognize both teammates and opponents for good gameplay is beneficial in a number of different ways. Whether players are encouraged to experiment with different play styles or just become more informed about how their teammates are contributing to their playing experience, when games encourage players to recognize each other's successes, everyone wins.

For Collaboration, Don't Let Players Talk to Each Other

LEE NEUSCHWANDER

You can expect players to interact in multiplayer games. Not all interactions are equal, though, and it's important to know the difference between the various types. Specifically, allowing players to interact with each other in a way that bolsters the continued experience of the game can be the difference between having a cooperative or a toxic community.

It's not just about letting players be nice to each other – how they can communicate matters. *Journey* is an adventure game in which you sometimes (often) run into another player. The game does not allow for any direct player communication. The only action you can perform, other than moving and jumping, is to "sing". When "singing", a sound plays and a unique-to-each-player icon appears above your head. Players quickly adopted the "singing", together with their character's movement, as a form of communication that encouraged collaboration in the game: helping a player to know where to go next, what to do, and so on. The singing is ambiguous and players have to try to both express an idea as well as interpret what the other player is doing. This takes time, and patience, and leads to a more collaborative and meaningful personal experience. After all, the second player is making an effort to help the other out!

One of the issues with direct communication is that players will sometimes use it to deliberately worsen another's experience, thus leading to a de-valuation of the entire communication system. *Dark Souls* has a messaging system that enables players to leave short messages that then appear in another player's game. However, the system is often used to troll new players with, for example, messages promising rewards for jumping off a cliff. Although the system gives players a way to warn others of potential risks further ahead or inform them of secrets they might have otherwise not found, a player that has fallen victim to a malicious message might not trust future messages. Thus, the whole system becomes tainted.

Effective communication is hard, but in games, adding a layer of ambiguity by preventing direct communication via text or chat means that players have to try to actively interpret another player's attempts at communicating. This can lead to more collaboration simply because players need to be more invested in communicating and interpreting each other's actions in the game.

Nothing feels better than playing a game and realizing that you belong to a large group of people who also greatly enjoy the game. It's an even better experience when such a group is actively cheering you on to get better at the game and improve your experience in a positive manner. Sometimes, no words is actually better!

Player Preferences Go Beyond Content and Gameplay

JACOB GRAHMANN

It is well known that different players like different things in their games. Some people might prefer action to strategy, or they might like shooting over puzzle solving. Player preferences extend beyond gameplay and mechanics to include content and themes. Similar to other media, some people might not like science fiction, preferring fantasy or horror instead. These differences in preferences include other things such as how, when and for what reasons it is valid to spend real-world currency in a game.

When *Star Wars Battlefront* II was released in 2017, there was some controversy regarding its monetization. *Star Wars Battlefront* II implemented some pay-to-win mechanics that allowed players to gain an upper hand by spending real-world money on in-game advantages. The developers were surprised by how this mechanic in their game was received in different parts of the world. While it was not well received by North American and European players, Chinese players had no issues or concerns. Broadly speaking, this was the result of different cultural norms. There are different ideas of what "fairness" is in these countries and there are also differences in expectations: it is common for Chinese games to have pay-to-play features.

It turns out that *what* people are accustomed to paying for can matter as much as how and when they pay for it. Context matters! While players may complain about a console games' micro-transactions, they won't be offended when playing games in an arcade. Paying $1.50 for a few minutes of gameplay in an arcade is fine, but the same amount for a permanent addition to a game (e.g. a new character in a fighting game) is viewed as offensive.

Knowing the player community that you are designing your game for is important for avoiding mistakes that could upset your target gaming audience. But, knowing their preferences and expectations regarding payment can be just as important. This is because gaming communities might have values that aren't expressed in game preferences.

Microtransaction "crate" options (Star Wars Battlefront II) (Image Source: gamerant.com)

Change Player Movement Speed to Encourage Collaboration

JOSÉ P. ZAGAL

In multiplayer collaborative games it can be a challenge to encourage players to stick together. Players have the tendency to wander off in opposite directions or to chase after different objectives. A solution that has been implemented in the past is to place limits on the maximum distance between player-controlled characters. Thus characters behave as if they were tied together. Another solution is to place limitations on the movement of the camera. So, if a character is at the top edge of the screen, it may not be able to move further upwards until the other arrives at that location, such that together they "free" the camera to continue moving.

While these solutions work, they are often perceived by players as heavy-handed or even intrusive. They can also have negative effects on gameplay – if, say, a character is unable to move closer to an enemy that is attacking it with a ranged attack, because their partner is stuck in another part of the level.

The adventure game *Journey* implements a novel solution that is subtle and also effective. It's not perfect in that it can't guarantee that two characters will remain close to each other, but it nudges characters toward this behavior. While *Journey* is nominally a single-player game, at different moments during the game another player's game may coincide with one's own. In these moments, two-players are co-located in the gameworld. How does *Journey* encourage them to stay reasonably close to each other? Well, it makes changes to how quickly the characters can move. Players' characters move slightly faster when moving towards each other, and slightly slower when moving away from each other. This makes it easier for characters to follow each other, and makes it harder for one character to run away and abandon the other. Thus, characters are subtly encouraged to stick together...making it easier for them to collaborate and help each other along.

Two players staying close together in Journey. (Image source: hookedgamers.com)

SKILLED PLAY

What do game designers do to help novice and expert players?

Hit Priority in Combat Systems Encourages Deeper and Competitive Play

JACOB GRAHMANN

Many games could benefit from implementing a hit priority system. A hit priority system assigns values to the different attacks within the game. This allows a move with a higher priority value to hit, instead of a move with lower values that was executed at the same time. By implementing this system, designers can create more complex fighting systems that reward players that take their time to learn how it works, while also increasing the number of options a player has.

For Honor is a multiplayer melee combat game that implements this feature. The game has multiple character classes, each with their own fighting style. During combat, players usually have three different stances, each with heavy and light attacks. When confronted with an opponent, players must choose both the appropriate combination of stances and attacks in order to beat their opponent. For example, the Warden character's light attacks are dangerous and have a high hit priority: if the Warden and another character simultaneously perform a light attack, the Warden's attack is likely to go through. Because of this, when playing against a Warden, players may tend to be less aggressive and wait for the Warden to attack first for a better advantage. Knowing which attacks will get priority over others is critical. Implementing a hit priority system in this way makes combat more interesting, it gives players more decisions in combat, it allows players to use moves situationally to counter opponents, and it forces players to think about their opponent and their decisions. This system makes the games' combat feel unique and rewards players who take the time to learn the habits and attack patterns that other players and characters use and prefer.

Hit priority systems can also reward players with quick reaction times. One game that does this is *PlayerUnknown's Battlegrounds*: if you are able to kill a player before their bullets hit you, their bullets will cease to do damage.

This rewards players who can shoot before their opponent by preventing the damage the player would receive from applying. Also, different weapons fire bullets that move at different speeds. So, if two players shoot each other at the same time, the one firing faster bullets will score the hit first and be safe (assuming they also kill their opponent). Faster bullets mean having higher priority shots. This leads to a system that rewards quicker fire more heavily than accurate fire, as in *Battlefield* 4, where each bullet fired will still apply damage, even after the player's death.

By tweaking small things, even the properties of bullets, developers can influence how competitive the game feels. If you know that your shots count even after your death, you are encouraged to give more attention to accuracy and aiming mechanics in the game. The mechanics of hit priority are a tool that can be used by many to spice up a dull combat system.

Original snack idea by Noah Harren.

Use Skill Trees to Enrich Your Players' Skills

KENDAL KOTTER

A skill tree is a kind of progression system. Traditionally, players earn "points" through play, which they then choose to spend to unlock "nodes" in the tree that grant bonuses or benefits. Each choice made also unlocks future choices – a tree with branches that fork into new branches. Skill trees can be used to purposefully gate content and naturally add new gameplay elements, all without overwhelming new players with complexity. They are also a great way to add variety and player customizability – they can empower players to play the game according to their own preferences and skills. More importantly, they can be used to help players develop and improve their skills at playing the game.

Assassin's Creed: Origins features a deep and varied skill tree with interweaving branches. Some of the abilities that can be unlocked encourage players to engage more deeply with the game's system – providing new skills for players to learn and master. For example, unlocking "Bow Bearer" adds a second bow to the player's ranged-weapon quick select system. This adds tactical options for players to discover and test – which two bows should you equip and how can you get the best use out of them? Similarly, the "Parry" option changes players' options in melee: they can now try to block attacks and follow up with a counter attack. To gain the most benefit from the skill tree option that was unlocked, the player needs to develop their own skills at the game. After all, if you don't learn how to parry and incorporate that into your combat skills, there's no sense in unlocking the skill.

If a skill tree balloons into a skill forest with many options, it can become too complex. This makes it harder to craft an interesting and engaging experience for the player since the more unlockable options you provide, the more likely it is for those options to be less meaningful and impactful to the play experience. Also, some games allow players to unlock every option on the tree by the end of the game. In this case, instead of forcing players to make difficult decisions about how they want to play the game, players are only deciding in what order they want to unlock content.

For a skill tree to enrich a player's skills at the game, it helps if the options unlocked grants players access to a new ability or item. A skill tree that unlocks an increase in a player's maximum health or enhances their punch attack by a certain percentage means little to players; it's a benefit, but not one that opens up new gameplay options or strategies, or demands that new skills be learned by players. *Dishonored* is another great example: its skill tree options grant players exciting new in-game abilities that are immediately useful and easily seen.

Many skill trees, including *Assassin's Creed: Origins*, have a mix of different unlocks – stat upgrades, abilities that are used automatically, as well as new abilities. Regardless, it should always be the case that players understand what they are unlocking and, if it's a new ability, understand how their gameplay options will be enriched.

Randomized Gun Spray Patterns Help Level the Playing Field for Players

BENJAMIN BARKER

Imagine firing a shotgun at a piece of paper. The resulting holes will form a pattern on the target. This is weapon spray, and different weapons have a different pattern. In games, the implementation of spray patterns affects a game's appeal to different types of players.

If one of the pillars of a game is mastery, having consistent spray is key. Predictable spray patterns teach players how to better aim a given weapon. If a gun always fires a closer concentration of bullets to the left, the player will know, when using that gun, to fire slightly to the right of the target. This rewards players who learn the game's weapon patterns. Rewarding such intimate knowledge of the game helps skilled players differentiate themselves from their competition. A skilled and knowledgeable player will always defeat the more casual player.

However, a consistent and predictable spray pattern may not always be the wisest. If a game is being developed for mass appeal, attracting a casual crowd is crucial. To avoid disenfranchising casual players who never stand a chance against skilled opponents, it is imperative to include some sort of in-game balancing mechanism. Allowing some of the spray to be random is one such mechanism. This means that the highly skilled player will miss more shots (due to randomness), while the casual player won't really notice (their aim is already poor): this evens them out a little.

We can see how this plays out in two popular first-person shooter games: *Counter Strike: Global Offensive* (CS:GO) and *Overwatch*. CS:GO has consistent and predictable spray patterns that vary from gun to gun, and experienced players learn the behaviors of each of the weapons to hone their skills. CS:GO's player base is smaller with most regular players interested in high-end competition play. While *Overwatch* has an active competitive scene, it also draws a large casual player base. *Overwatch*'s spray patterns can hardly be called patterns. Most of its guns fire in largely random trajectories along or near the crosshairs. This lowers the barrier for entry, as players do not need to learn spray patterns to have a fighting chance in online matchups.

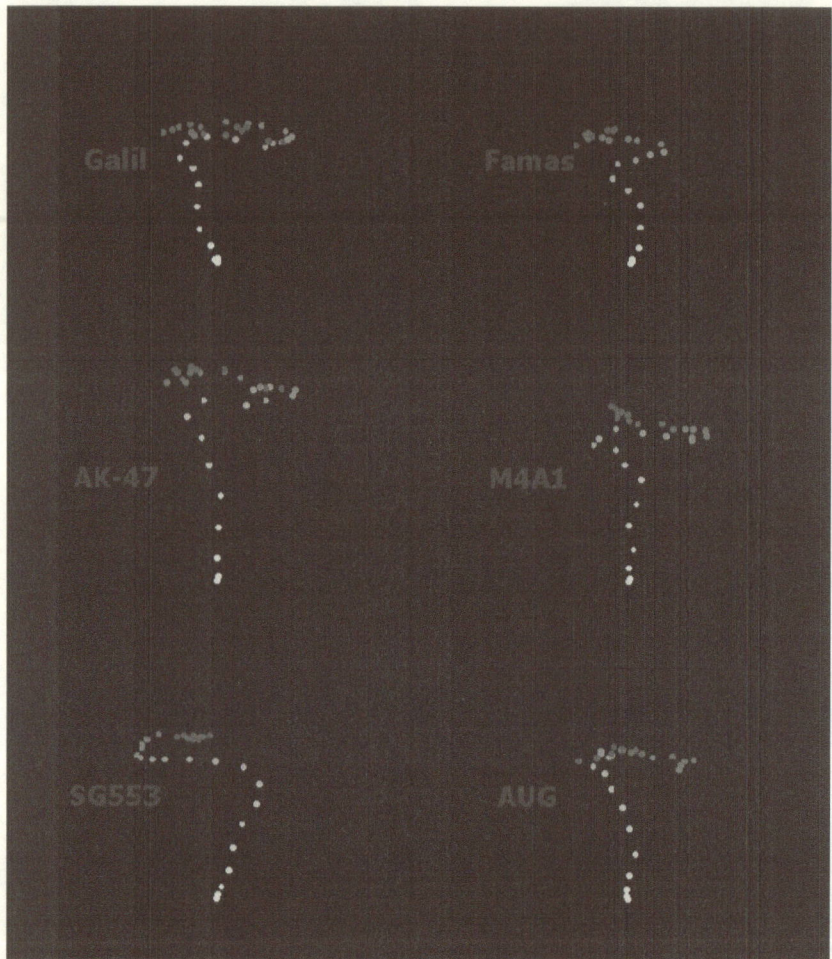

Spray patterns of different weapons (Counter Strike: Global Offensive)

The lesson here is that randomness can level the playing field between players and adjusting spray patterns is one easy way to do so.

Original snack idea by Tanden Peterson.

Layer your Design to Achieve Both a Low Skill Floor and a High Skill Ceiling

KENDAL KOTTER

Designing a game with a high skill ceiling (where players must invest significant time and effort to achieve maximum skill) often results in a game with a relatively high skill floor as well. This leads to situations where newcomers are essentially gated away from enjoying the game; the game's intended playability is only accessible after clearing the skill floor. Conversely, designing a game with a low skill floor often leads to a similarly low skill ceiling, generally due to lack of complexity and player choices (i.e. Tic-Tac-Toe). How can the positive aspects of both of these approaches – namely, a plethora of player choices and depth, as well as accessibility to less-skilled players – be designed into a single game?

The answer is lenticular (or layered) design. The term, coined by Mark Rosewater, head designer for collectible card game *Magic: The Gathering* (*MtG*), comes from lenticular printing which is a technique where multiple images are combined with a lenticular lens, such that the final image changes depending on the angle it's viewed from. In *MtG*, this type of design is applied when certain cards are easily and immediately understood by beginning players, while simultaneously containing a hidden complexity that can be taken advantage of and used by more experienced players. This results in situations where both beginning and expert players can enjoy the same cards, but at different levels of play. This same technique can be applied to videogames.

Many fighting games employ lenticular design. One example is *Super Smash Bros.*, a game that is known for being marketed to casual gamers, while still enjoying a high rate of competitive play. The game is successful because players can quickly pick up a controller and understand how to play on a basic level. Their actions result in consequences that are both understandable and satisfying (i.e. punching is enjoyable due to immediate feedback of action and reaction, jumping is natural and intuitive, etc.). Casual players can enjoy the game and be successful at it without needing to understand complex strategies or mechanics. However, *Super Smash Bros.* is chock-full of complexity, both mechanically and strategically, that allows a much deeper level of play. The player community has identified what they call "Advanced Techniques" that are difficult to perform, requiring high precision and technical skills when playing the game. Edge dashing and cancelling, fox-trotting, and pivoting are just a few examples. This allows for a game that is designed for both novices and casual players, as well as experts and professional gamers.

Although it might not be easy to do, lenticular design can be appropriately applied to mass appeal games (i.e. games with a general audience, instead of a specific one). Overall, we can summarize this design philosophy as one that can lead to games that are easy to learn, but challenging to master.

Let Experienced Players Turn Off Breadcrumbs

LEE NEUSCHWANDER

In the fairy tale, Hansel and Gretel, two kids get lost in the woods after birds eat a trail of bread crumbs they had been dropping behind them with the intention of following them home once they were done exploring in the woods. This idea has made its way into videogames, with game designers often placing items of interest such that they encourage players to move in certain directions or towards certain features in the environment. Breadcrumbs for the player to follow can be useful, but there are also drawbacks.

Breadcrumbs can discourage players from exploring environments on their own, taking away some of the fun of a game experience. They might also prove distracting and reduce immersion – especially when they are represented in the game in unrealistic ways like trails of sparkling lights in an otherwise real-world-based game. Furthermore, if navigation is a skill being challenged in a game, breadcrumbs can help with learning to navigate, but afterwards become useless: at this point what the player wants is a new challenge to master.

A small change in the design can make all the difference, however: what if the breadcrumb trail was optional? With optional breadcrumbs, designers still retain the ability to ease new players in while taking away an unwanted feature of the game for those who don't need it.

Scout Flies leading hunter to the monster (Monster Hunter World) (Image Source: game.capscon.com)

One example of breadcrumbs being used well is in *Monster Hunter World*. In this game there are creatures called Scoutflies, which will help point players in the direction of the monster they are tasked with hunting. However, players can opt to ignore these breadcrumbs as they will only show up if they are set to track the monster. There are also plenty of ways for more experienced players to know where the monster is located, without needing the Scoutflies for aid. For a game that's fundamentally about tracking and killing monsters, being able to play as a "true" hunter makes for a more engaging experience, while still allowing players to manage their own difficulty level by using Scoutflies when they want to. This concept is also used in many racing games where it's called a racing line – a virtual line that is overlaid on a race track indicating the optimal route for a driver to take on a course. They are often optional as well, and are a great tool for players to learn how to best race on a given track.

Original snack idea by Ian Rappleye.

Index of Games

A

Alien: Isolation   19-20

Assassin's Creed: Origins   107-108

B

Bastion   55

Battlefield   78

Battlefield 4   106

Bioshock Infinite   13

Bloodborne   91

Breath of Fire IV   69

C

Call of Duty   42, 78

Castlevania: Symphony of the Night   33

Celeste   56, 61-62

Civilization IV   33

Counter Strike: Global Offensive   109-110

Crash Bandicoot   78

D

Dark Souls   7, 23, 30, 33, 37, 97

Dishonored   48, 108

Doki Doki Literature Club   15-16

Doom   42

Door Kickers   79-80

F

Firewatch   75

For Honor   105

Fortnite   86

G

Gears of War   78

Getting Over It   41

God of War   36, 87

H

Halo   42

Heavy Rain   13, 74

Hellblade: Senua's Sacrifice   75-76

Horizon Zero Dawn   89-90

I

Infamous 2   81–82

Into the Breach   5–6

J

Journey   35–36, 97, 101–102

L

Last of Us, The   19

Legend of Zelda, The (Series)   3, 77

- – *Breath of the Wild* 51
- – *Link to the Past, A* 77
- – *Majora's Mask* 77
- – *Ocarina of Time* 77
- – *Twilight Princess* 7–8

League of Legends   95

Little Big Planet   42

M

Magic: The Gathering   111

Metroid   33, 86

Metroid Prime   69

Middle Earth: Shadow of War   67

Minecraft   86

Monster Hunter World   114

Mortal Kombat   86

O

Overwatch   25, 95-96, 109

P

PlayerUnknown's Battlegrounds   25, 105

Pyre   56

R

Rayman Legends   65

Resident Evil   41-42

Rise of the Tomb Raider   18

Rogue Legacy   59-60

S

SCP – Containment Breach   27

Shadow of the Tomb Raider   18

Silent Hill   42

Silent Hill 2   28

Skyrim   39, 91

Soulcalibur 6   9

Spider-Man   3, 62, 90

Stanley Parable, The   16

Star Wars Battlefront II   99-100

Street Fighter   86

Super Mario Bros   85

Super Mario Odyssey   49-50, 85

Super Mario Sunshine   82, 85

Super Meat Boy   25-26

Super Smash Bros   111-112

T

Team Fortress 2   53

Tom Clancy's The Division   45

Tomb Raider   18

U

Uncharted   78

Uncharted: Drake's Fortune   65

Undertale   67

Until Dawn   87-88

W

Witcher, The (Series)   17

Witcher 3, The   63

Witness, The   91

World of Warcraft   53, 63

About the Authors

Benjamin Barker

Benjamin Barker has a Bachelor degree in English and a Masters in Entertainment Arts and Engineering, both from the University of Utah. He is passionate about interactive storytelling, dogs, and world travel.

McKenna Caldwell

McKenna was born and raised in Salt Lake City, Utah. She became fascinated with the immersive storytelling capabilities of games as a young child. She enjoys meeting new people and is always searching for her next adventure.

Jacob Grahmann

Jacob grew up in Sandy, Utah, and came to love nature during his childhood. Along with hiking and hunting, some of his other hobbies include a strong passion for PC gaming, and spending time with his special needs cat. Jacob's favorite way to relax when finished with work is to play games with his friends.

Kendal Kotter

Kendal Kotter is a game developer from small town Idaho whose work centers around narrative and UI design. He is committed to promoting empathy, inclusivity, and diversity within his work. Along with game development, Kendal is also passionate about interactive fiction, cats, and his quest to bake the perfect pie.

Lee Neuschwander

Lee was born in 1996 and was raised in Woods Cross, Utah. He grew up enjoying games on the Playstation, Xbox, Gameboy Color, and Nintendo 64. Since he first played a video game, Halo on the Xbox, he has been fascinated with the idea of having such games be a part of his life. Lee first became involved with the games industry when he started college in 2015 with the EAE program at the University of Utah. With a focus in level design, Lee is driven to create games that capture players in unique and engaging worlds.

Trevor Scott Richard

Trevor Scott Richard is a game designer and writer who has been playing video-games too much since before he could read, and intends to continue doing so until his time on Earth is up. His greatest ambition in life is to empirically demonstrate that we are all living in a Matrix-like simulation, and his favorite food is mint chocolate chip ice-cream.

José Zagal

José Zagal is faculty at the University of Utah's top-ranked game development program. He wrote "Ludoliteracy" and edited the "Videogame Ethics Reader" and "Role-Playing Game Studies". He was also honored as a distinguished game scholar by the digital games research association (DiGRA). He also likes games. A lot.

About the ETC Press

The ETC Press was founded in 2005 under the direction of Dr. Drew Davidson, the Director of Carnegie Mellon University's Entertainment Technology Center (ETC), as an open access, digital-first publishing house.

What does all that mean?

The ETC Press publishes three types of work:peer-reviewed work (research-based books, textbooks, academic journals, conference proceedings), general audience work (trade nonfiction, singles, Well Played singles), and research and white papers

The common tie for all of these is a focus on issues related to entertainment technologies as they are applied across a variety of fields.

Our authors come from a range of backgrounds. Some are traditional academics. Some are practitioners. And some work in between. What ties them all together is their ability to write about the impact of emerging technologies and its significance in society.

To distinguish our books, the ETC Press has five imprints:

- **ETC Press:** our traditional academic and peer-reviewed publications;
- **ETC Press: Single:** our short "why it matters" books that are roughly 8,000-25,000 words;
- **ETC Press: Signature:** our special projects, trade books, and other curated works that exemplify the best work being done;
- **ETC Press: Report:** our white papers and reports produced by practitioners or academic researchers working in conjunction with partners; and
- **ETC Press: Student:** our work with undergraduate and graduate students

In keeping with that mission, the ETC Press uses emerging technologies to design all of our books and Lulu, an on-demand publisher, to distribute our e-books and print books through all the major retail chains, such as Amazon,

Barnes & Noble, Kobo, and Apple, and we work with The Game Crafter to produce tabletop games.

We don't carry an inventory ourselves. Instead, each print book is created when somebody buys a copy.

Since the ETC Press is an open-access publisher, every book, journal, and proceeding is available as a free download. We're most interested in the sharing and spreading of ideas. We also have an agreement with the Association for Computing Machinery (ACM) to list ETC Press publications in the ACM Digital Library.

Authors retain ownership of their intellectual property. We release all of our books, journals, and proceedings under one of two Creative Commons licenses:

- **Attribution-NoDerivativeWorks-NonCommercial:** This license allows for published works to remain intact, but versions can be created; or
- **Attribution-NonCommercial-ShareAlike:** This license allows for authors to retain editorial control of their creations while also encouraging readers to collaboratively rewrite content.

This is definitely an experiment in the notion of publishing, and we invite people to participate. We are exploring what it means to "publish" across multiple media and multiple versions. We believe this is the future of publication, bridging virtual and physical media with fluid versions of publications as well as enabling the creative blurring of what constitutes reading and writing.